A Devotional Study Series

M000020555

UNRIVALED: PASSION OF
One

LEARNING TO LIVE LOVED IN GOD

The One-Series
Volume Two

EMPOWERED WOMEN'S MINISTRIES
Pentecostal Church of God

pcg.org/women

WOMEN'S MINISTRIES
PENTECOSTAL CHURCH OF GOD

UNRIVALED: PASSION OF ONE Learning to Live Loved By God Devotional, The One series, vol. 2. Copyright ©2020 Annual Devotional by Empowered Women's Ministries of the Pentecostal Church of God, 2701 Brown Trail, Suite 500, Bedford, Texas 76021—pcg.org/women

Editor in Chief: Kimberly Ming
Editor: Laura Salazar
Design and Layout: Department of Women's Ministries and Kimberly Ming
Layout Editor: Spencer Ming
Photography by:
      Emily Herndon @emilyyherndonn- Front cover; page 5, 14; chapter covers 1, 3, 4, 6, 9, 11; and the back cover

Printed in the United States of America

First Printing, January 2020

www.pcg.org/women

ISBN: 9781656710420

This book was written with you in mind and
is dedicated to every empowered woman
who is passionately loved by God.
YES, THAT WOULD BE YOU!

HOW TO USE THIS BOOK

Unrivaled: Passion of One is designed to be versatile and easy to use. When delving into these studies, you will find there are multiple ways to apply the information!

This can be read as a personal Bible study or used to mentor another woman. You can go through it informally with friends. Or it could easily be utilized as the curriculum for a small group, since it is designed complete with discussion questions. The content can even be used in a large group setting for topical teaching or preaching.

The timeline is also flexible: It can be a 12-day (once a day), 12-week (once a week), or 12-month (once a month) study guide!

This beautifully designed devotional study book includes twelve devotions that you will love, and there are twelve themed topics and key Scripture verses. Each session also includes:

- **Ask Yourself** – Following each devotion, you will find personal application questions that will reflect back to what you just read.

- **Digging Deeper** – For those that want a deeper understanding of what the Word of God says on the given topic, *"Digging Deeper"* leads the reader on a journey into Scripture and questions of the text.

- **Personal Application**– A personal challenge to help apply what has been learned.

- **Prayer Activation**– Apply what has been learned through prayer.

- **Love Notes**– Don't forget what you've learned and what the Holy Spirit has been saying to you. There is plenty of space to journal those sweet love note thoughts at the end of each session.

The margins in this devotional are wide so you have plenty of space to answer questions, write out thoughts or Scripture, and/or add your own creative doodle artwork.

We ask that you think about using this devotional as a resource to pour into another woman or a group of women. This devotional will also serve as a great gift for a friend, your pastor's wife, or a missionary.

To order more, CONTACT us at:
empoweredwmin@pcg.org

UNRIVALED PASSION OF | *One*

CONTENTS

INTRODUCTION:
From the Director

Once again, I am very excited to introduce a new devotional, this time with the theme and title— **UNRIVALED: PASSION OF ONE.** A couple of years ago the Lord impressed on my heart that we needed more than just one devotional study focused on our relationship with God. Instead, I felt like we needed a trilogy which emphasized the ONE God.

In 2019, we studied the Unlimited Power of One, and over twelve chapters, we were inspired to rekindle our intimate connection with God and others. Now, in this second book in the series, our hope is that we will discover the unrivaled love of God and develop intimate relationship with Him as a result.

In a culture obsessed with using the word "love," the definition of love has been so compressed that it has become a very casual word used over and over in a days' time. People are addicted to love. It is common to describe love in the same context as pizza and Hallmark movies. But it is also stretched to produce deadly lies and false emotions. In a society that has made "love" both common and perverted, it is vitally important that we, as the body of Christ, understand what true love is. We need to understand that God is love and that He is the very definition of the truest, purest kind of love. We are often so busy looking for another feeling or an emotional high, but God's love is not a feeling or an emotion. It is truth.

God's desire is to lavish His love on all of us—you and I both. He desires that we know He is passionately in love with us. His love can literally and radically change your whole life, since perceptions and perspectives all change when we understand how much we are loved. When we know we are loved by God, we won't settle for anything other than the real deal– God's unrivaled love.

God's love is unrivaled because there is nothing else that can match it. No other love can compete with it or come close to it. There is no other love that has sacrificed any more, given any more, promised any more. There is no other love that is perfect, that never fails, never leaves, never abandons. There is no other love that can always be trusted and will always do what is best. Oh, there is no love or passion like God's love for us. It is on every level and in every description completely and totally unrivaled!

As I have studied the Scriptures over the years, Gods love has jumped off the pages, book after book and chapter after chapter. He has showed Himself to me as a loving Father and passionate Groom time and time again. As I spoke to the other talented authors who collaborated in writing these devotions, they too have experienced God's love in such incredible ways, and we all are so glad to share what the Lord has been revealing to us.

> In a society that has made "love" both common and perverted, it is vitally important that we understand what **true love** is.

I am confident that this devotional will be a blessing to you and your friends because God has been in it since its inception. The thoughts, devotions, and creativity have all come from Him with you in mind. Each session has been covered in prayer with the desire that you will not only know that you are loved, but that you will radically and passionately **LIVE LOVED.** In a day and time when the world has redefined love as empty and fake, there has never been a better time for us to rise up and proclaim the purity of a love that rings true.

So, get with your sisterhood, your girl tribe, your empowered friends. Grab your Bible and a good cup of coffee or tea. Get ready to dig deep into God's Word and let God's Unrivaled Passion pour over you!

Serving the ONE,

Kimberly Ming

Kimberly Ming
Empowered Women's Ministries Director
Pentecostal Church of God

MEET THE
CONTRIBUTORS:

Face to Beautiful Face...

DEVOTIONAL CONTRIBUTORS-

Session 1: LOVE REDEFINED

1. *Sula Skiles* is a pastor, author, and sex trafficking abolitionist. Her passion for ministry stems from overcoming a very painful past. As a survivor of sex trafficking, she works to spread awareness, teach prevention, and help victims and survivors. She has written two books: *Fighting for Your Purpose* and *His Beloved Bride—A Journey into Deeper Intimacy with Jesus*. Sula is happily married to Pastor John Mark Skiles. Together, they are church planters (having started Impact Life Church in Destin, Florida), and they are incredibly blessed to have two beautiful children.

Session 2: LOVE CHOOSES

2. *Darla Skiles* has been in full-time ministry for 20 years. She is passionate about empowering leaders, sharing truth, and helping people become the best version of themselves. Darla is the founder of She Tribe, believing + becoming women's ministry. She currently lives in Jefferson City, Missouri, where she serves as executive pastor at Solid Rock Church. She has been married to her husband, Tom, for 24 years and is the mother of Gavin and Abby Skiles (two pretty amazing young adults).

Session 3: LOVE RESTORES

3. *Devorah Robinson* is passionate about encouraging women to live out their potential and to find their divine purpose. She currently leads a ministry called "Women with Purpose," a support group for women who have experienced the devastating effects of domestic violence. She has a master's degree in educational counseling from Cal Lutheran University. Devorah is blessed to be married to her amazing, loving husband and best friend, Robby. She loves going on vacations and creating memories with him. They currently reside in Valencia, California, and serve at Higher Vision Church.

Session 4: LOVE TRUSTS

4. *Kathryn Wenth* loves the Body of Christ and encourages those around her to live their lives pursuing Jesus! She has pastored as an ordained minister for 13 years and has spent the last five years as an associate pastor of the Pastoral Care Ministry at New Life Family Church in Euless, Texas. Kathryn has been married to an amazing man for 46 years, and they have seven children who, along with their spouses, have given them 15 grandchildren. Her favorite thing: family vacation at the beach.

Session 5: LOVE SERVES

5. *Rebecca Pickett* homeschools her six kids and hosts many visitors in her home and guest house. She and her husband, Grady, are Pentecostal Church of God missionaries to the Middle East and Iraq. They currently pastor a thriving house church in Erbil, Kurdistan, and help refugees. Becky loves gathering friends and family at her big farmhouse table, where they share delicious food, great coffee, and spirited conversations.

Session 6: LOVE WAITS

6. *Mary Price* was born and raised in the small town of Arlington, Ohio. She grew up in church and has served in several capacities. She attended college at Bowling Green State University in Ohio and received her BA in business management. She currently serves as part of the World Missions Department administrative team at the Pentecostal Church of God International Mission Center in Bedford, Texas. Mary also serves on the worship team at New Life Family Church in Euless, Texas. She loves sports, spending time with family and friends, and traveling.

Session 7: LOVE CONNECTS

7. *Kathleen Smith* is a high school math teacher in south Dallas and is involved in ministry through her local church. She has a Bachelor of Arts in Education and is currently pursuing a master's degree in organizational leadership through Southwestern Assemblies of God University. Kat has a passion for equipping people to discover their God-given purpose, seeing racism end, and helping women understand their place as daughters of God. She loves lifting weights, matcha lattes, and quality conversations.

Session 8: LOVE COVERS

8. *Darlene Rhodes* serves as co-lead pastor with her husband, Darryl, at Solid Rock Church in Farmington, Missouri. She travels internationally, speaking for WAW Conferences (Women Around the World Ministries.) She has experienced miracles firsthand and often says that God took her "not enough" and made it "more than enough!" Darlene's personal story is shared in her autobiography entitled *The Miracle of The Breaking*. She loves spending time with her family, pastoring, and having coffee in unique coffee shops around the globe with the love of her life, Darryl!

Session 9: LOVE SHOWS UP

9. *Beverly Hylton* is co-lead pastor for Bethel Family Worship Center in Indianapolis, Indiana, where she has served alongside her husband, Rev. Russell Hylton, for the past 20 years. She is passionate about seeing women of all ages walk into their God-given destiny. She has been married to her high school sweetheart for 28 years. They have a daughter and son-in-law who are parents to their precious first grandchild, Liam Elijah. Beverly enjoys traveling, reading, and home décor.

Session 10: LOVE LIFTS

10. *Angela Foster* has been married and in active ministry for 25 years. She pastors alongside her Army chaplain husband, James, and they have led multiple congregations across the United States and overseas while raising three wonderful children. Angela has enjoyed mentoring and encouraging military spouses and families for over 18 years. She has been active in many ladies' groups and co-taught small groups, but she thrives in mentoring one on one. God has used Angela to speak into the lives of ladies through their suffering, pain, and personal growth. She considers it an honor to be called to serve military families and share the Word of God.

Session 11: LOVE GROWS

11. *Julie Lester* has served by her husband, James, in ministry for the past 25 years- first in church ministry and then as an active duty army spouse. With their three children, they have had an adventure of a lifetime, already living in more than ten states and in the process of moving overseas for their next assignment. Julie left her first career as a teacher to raise her children and serve God and country. She is currently in seminary working on a master's degree in biblical studies. Julie feels this is something bigger than herself, which can only be accomplished because of God's prodding and power.

Session 12: LOVE EXTENDS

12. *Micah Yursik* and her husband, Taylor, are missionaries in the Amazon Jungle of Peru. They also serve stateside in Bakersfield, California, running a missionary training school called the Antioch Center. Micah and Taylor have been married for four years. During this time, they have both received their Bachelor of Arts degrees in Biblical Studies with an emphasis in Global Missions plus completed one-year immersive mission internships in Central America. They know they are called by God to reach His Amazon Bride while raising up an end-time army of missionaries! Micah loves to do ministry with her family, eat KitKats and hot Cheetos while watching movies, play with new makeup, laugh, write songs...and she loves to preach the Word of God!

QUESTIONS AND OTHER CONTENT CONTRIBUTORS-

13. *Kimberly Ming* is the National Director of Empowered Women's Ministries for the Pentecostal Church of God. She has a heart to encourage others to passionately pursue a relationship with God and find their purpose where they have been placed. She is an ordained minister with the PCG and a graduate of Messenger College with a B.A. in Biblical Studies. She has served along side her husband as lead-pastors, as a District Women's Ministries Director, and as the assistant to two PCG General Secretaries. She also started a successful interior design business in California, connecting the application of ministry to everyday life. Kimberly has been crazy in love and married to her husband, Dr. Wayman Ming Jr., for thirty years. He currently serves as the General Bishop of the PCG, and together, they reside in Fort Worth, Texas, and have three children and a daughter-in-love: Spencer, Justice, Garrett, and Grace.

14. *Ashlynn Hunley* is from Indiana, but is now living in Euless, Texas to attend Messenger College. She currently serves as the Empowered Women's Ministries Assistant and as the Student Body President for Messenger College where she is pursuing a Bachelors in Christian Ministries with an emphasis in Student Ministries and a minor in Biblical Studies. Her passions include worship, leadership, camps, and kids ministry. She desires to teach and raise up the next generation of leaders to further build the Kingdom of God and help others in their walk with Jesus. Ashlynn also enjoys exploring new places and discovering new things, especially if it includes friends and a good cup of coffee.

"**I** am convinced that nothing can ever separate us from

God's Love.

neither death nor life,

neither angels nor demons,

neither our fears for today

nor our worries about tomorrow-

Not even the powers of hell

can separate us from God's love.

No power in the sky

above or in the earth below-

indeed, nothing in all creation

will ever be able to separate us

from the love of God

that is revealed in

Christ Jesus our Lord.

Romans 8:38-39 (NLT)

_____

Love: Redefined
Transformed by the Bridegroom!

Sula Skiles—

*"For you reach into my heart. With one flash of your eyes I am undone
by your love, my beloved, my equal, my bride. You leave me breathless—
I am overcome by merely a glance from your worshiping eyes, for you
have stolen my heart. I am held hostage by your love and by the graces
of righteousness shining upon you. How satisfying to me, my equal, my bride.
Your love is my finest wine—intoxicating and thrilling. And your sweet,
perfumed praises—so exotic, so pleasing."*
Song of Solomon 4:9-10 (TPT)

Now that, ladies, is how Jesus feels about us! Wild and crazy, right? Our ability to be loved is not defined by how people feel about us or what the world says about us. *We are defined by what Jesus feels and says about us.* All throughout the Bible, there are Scriptures about our marriage covenant with the Lord. One of my favorite books is Song of Songs (Solomon), which illustrates the beautiful love relationship between Jesus and us as the Bride. In fact, my favorite thing in the world to listen to is The Passion Translation audio-obook of Song of Songs. It's like listening to how Jesus, our First Love Forever, feels about us over and over again.

For several years, I understood the concept of "Jesus as my Husband" in head knowledge. I'd read the Scriptures many times and thought I knew what it meant to be His Beloved Bride. However, I wasn't living from that joy-filled and love-drenched reality on a daily basis. Then, a hunger for the longings in my soul to be satisfied propelled me into *bridal* encounters with Jesus. This jolted me from head knowledge to divine, intimate revelation. His Bridegroom love transformed me. I was pretty comfortable with the idea that I was radically in love with Him. Jesus rescued me from many traumas in my life including sexual abuse, physical violence, sex trafficking, addiction, eating disorders, depression, suicide attempts... just to name a few. So, of course He had all my devotion, attention, and affection. However, understanding how obsessively and passionately in love He is with me—that was a whole new adventure to explore. After all that I had been through, how could He actually love me that much?

His Bridegroom love transformed me...
His love began Redefining me.

Redefined by Love
His love began redefining me. Through the bridal revelation, I discovered that not only are we completely undone by His love, but He is undone by ours (as seen in the key verse above). When we truly understand what it means to be His Beloved, we daily experience His affections lavished upon us. The emptiest and most hopeless places in our hearts are healed, and they begin to overflow with Him. How is it possible for the one who is so holy, holy, holy to desire us as His Bride?

"When he had sipped the sour wine, he said, "It is finished, my bride!" Then he bowed his head and surrendered his spirit to God."
—John 19:30 (TPT)

The last words of Jesus on the Cross were to us, His Bride. The Hebrew word *kalah* means completed or finished, and it also means BRIDE. When Jesus died on the cross, it was not only so that we could be saved, set free, and physically and emotionally healed; it was also so that we could become a pure bride. Through His sacrifice for us, we are invited into deep intimacy with Him as our Bridegroom King Lover with no veil of separation between. The veil in the temple that separated the Holy of Holies was torn from top to bottom when Jesus gave up His life on the cross (Matthew 27:51). This means that we can encounter our Husband, the King of Glory, at any time. We can run boldly before the throne of grace uncovered, with no shame, condemnation, or guilt. Jesus died for His Bride and we were on His mind when He took His last breath. That's an unrivaled kind of passionate love.

Thank God that our ability to experience this passionate love relationship with Jesus is not dependent on our religious, legalistic works but on the power of the cross. His love opened the door for us to be able to encounter Him as our lover in a very real and tangible way. There is nothing in our human strength that we could ever do to earn this love from Jesus, the Bridegroom King. It is all through Him and for His Glory. It is time for us to live as the Bride of Christ, from the ascended reality of being seated in heavenly realms with Him (Ephesians 2:6).

> *We are no longer fearful victims; orphans; powerless, defeated soldiers; or rejected, beaten down slaves under harsh task masters...*
> *We are the glorious Bride of Christ*
> *And we are dearly **loved, empowered,** and forever **adored** by Him!*

Our perspective on how we handle challenging situations, persecution, suffering, and attacks is so different as the Bride. We get to live in the authority of our Husband and His Name. We are no longer fearful victims; orphans; powerless, defeated soldiers; or rejected, beaten-down slaves under harsh task masters—we are redefined by His love. We are the glorious Bride of Christ, and we are dearly loved, empowered, and forever adored by Him.

For more information on the Bride of Christ, read Sula's new book:
His Beloved Bride– A Journey Into Deeper Intimacy with Jesus
Available on Amazon

What are the primary ways Jesus has been revealed to you in the past?
(Examples: savior, friend, father, healer, teacher, etc.) Ask Him to take you into deeper love encounters.

Have you ever had an emptiness in your heart that Jesus filled? How?
(Reflect on the ways Jesus filled and healed your heart through His love.)

Search your heart. Is there an area of your life you need the Bridegroom King Lover Jesus to come into? (Actively invite Him into that place.)

How does knowing that God thinks of you as the bride of Christ change your mind set about how you should view yourself?

Digging Deeper:

Read Ephesians 2:1-10. Complete verse 1.

"As for you, you were _____ in your transgressions and sins."

According to these verses we were all dead in sin. We were seeking love by gratifying the cravings of the flesh and following after our own earthly desires, thoughts, and pleasures. We lived as rebellious children deserving of God's wrath.

Instead of the wrath or discipline that we deserve, according to verses 4-5, describe the reaction God has toward us.

According to verses 6-7, when we are saved by Christ, how does our position change? Where are you lifted? Where are you seated?

According to verses 8-10, what do we have to do or achieve to earn the love of God?

There is nothing that we can do to achieve His love. We are loved! We must learn how to receive His love and be transformed by it. Jesus is not like people. He will not lie to us, cheat on us, talk down to us harshly, reject us, withhold affection from us, or manipulate us. His love is so much higher than man's earthly love.

Read Isaiah 55:8-9.
What does Isaiah say about the thoughts and ways of God?

If His ways are higher, His love must be higher.
If His thoughts are higher, His love thoughts toward you are also higher.

Read Psalm 139:17-18 and Jeremiah 29:11.
Describe God's true thoughts toward you?

When we lie down at night, and when we wake up in the morning, God's thoughts are constantly lavished upon us! His thoughts are of His cherished Bride.

Throughout Scripture, Christ has been defined as the Bridegroom, and we have been redefined as His Bride. Take a moment to read the following Scriptures and meditate on the truth of the Word. Ask Jesus to speak to your heart about how His love redefines you as His Bride.

John 3:29-30 (TPT)

"John answered…. 'He is the Bridegroom, and the bride belongs to him. I am the friend of the Bridegroom who stands nearby and listens with great joy to the Bridegroom's voice. And because of his words my joy is complete and overflows! So, it's necessary for him to increase and for me to be diminished.'"

These were the words used by John the Baptist to describe Jesus (the long awaited Messiah) as the Bridegroom and the church as His Bride.

Why was it so important for the old covenant to diminish John the Baptist?

How was our love covenant redefined?

2 Corinthians 11:2 (TPT)

"You need to know that God's passion is burning inside me for you, because, like a loving father, I have pledged your hand in marriage to Christ, your true bridegroom. I've also promised that I would present his fiancée to Him as a pure virgin bride."

As Paul is writing to the Corinthian church, he describes himself as a father. He has been their spiritual father—loving, mentoring, and teaching them the things of God.

What does Paul say is burning inside him? What was Paul so passionate about?

How does God's love redefine us into a place of purity as a virgin bride?

Revelation 19:7-8 (TPT)

"Let us rejoice and exalt him and give him glory, because the wedding celebration of the Lamb has come. And his bride has made herself ready. Fine linen, shining bright and clear, has been given to her to wear, and the fine linen represents the righteous deeds of his holy believers."

Our entry into Heaven is a wedding celebration. How are you preparing yourself as the Bride?

Matthew 22:2-4 *(Please read the entire parable.)*

After reading this revelation in its entirety (Matthew 22:2-14), what does this explanation of the Kingdom realm say to you about reaching and inviting others into a love relationship with Jesus as the Bride?

Read Revelation 22:17

How can you increase your hunger and longing for the coming of Jesus as shown here in the last chapter of the Bible?

Personal Application:

What are the main ways that you encounter the love of Jesus each day?
(Examples: hearing His voice, seeing visions and dreams, inner knowing/ sensing, reading the word, worship, etc.)

Ask Jesus to reveal His true and passionate love toward you in new and deeper ways, while allowing Him to redefine all of your old, earthly concepts of love. Ask Him to activate all the ways that you can have new life-redefining bridal encounters with Him.

Prayer Activation: *(Please read out loud.)*

Lord Jesus,
Thank You for redefining how I see love and redefining me through Your love. I invite You to come...I ask that You reveal Yourself to me as my Bridegroom King Lover and Husband. Open my eyes of understanding and open my ears to hear what the Spirit of the Lord is saying to me. Quicken and awaken my heart to encounter You in new ways. Jesus, I want to see Your face and tangibly experience Your presence and Your affections for me. I renounce any lies that I've learned about Your love for me through emotional pain of my past. Tear down any walls or blocks that cause me to feel separated or distant from You. I forgive anyone who has demonstrated a false, toxic example of love to me in the past. I release them from everything they owe me. I turn away from every idol, every other "lover" that seeks to take my attention off of You. I give You, Jesus, all my attention, my love, and my adoration. Help me to encounter You in the deepest places of intimacy. Take me into Your glorious throne room. I am Your beloved and You are mine.
Amen.

Love Redefined

Our daily used language doesn't allow for full expression of the meaning of love, but the ancient Greeks named the differences with more clarity. Love, deserves to be fully understood in every way.

GREEK- DEFINED LOVE

AGAPE [*ah - gah - pey*] — The highest and most radical type of love according to the Greeks is *agape*, or unconditional love.

LUDUS [*lu - dus*] — The Greeks thought of *ludus* as a playful form of love; for example, the affection between children or the feeling that accompanies the early stages of falling in love with someone.

STORGE [*stor – gey*] — Often considered to be the love shared among family, *storge*, or familiar love, has to do with kinship and familiarity.

EROS [*er – os*] — Named for the Greek god of love and fertility, *eros*, or erotic love, is a passionate form of love that arouses romantic and sexual feelings.

PRAGMA [*prag – mah*] — *Pragma*, or enduring love, has aged, matured, and developed over time.

PHILIA [*fil – ee – ah*] — The ancient Greeks valued *philia*, or affectionate love, because it was considered a love between equals—a deep, meaningful friendship.

The most perfect definition of Love is described in the Bible. This is a love that is unrivaled and completely like no other.

BIBLE– RE-DEFINED LOVE

LOVE (REDEFINED) - **"GOD IS LOVE!"**

"Beloved, let us love one another, for Love is of God; and everyone who loves is born of God and knows God. He who does not love does not know God, for God is Love. In this the love of God was manifested toward us, that God has sent His only begotten Son into the world, that we might live through Him. In this love, not that we love God, but that He Loved Us and sent His Son to be the propitiation of our sins. Beloved, if God so loved us, we also ought to love one another...And we have known and believed the love that God has for us. God is Love, and he who abides in love abides in God, and God in him...
*We love Him because **HE FIRST LOVED US**."*

1 John 4:8-11, 16, 19 (NKJV)

To my Bride,

_____

(insert your name)

I love you more than words can express. I have given you my Son, so you may not perish but have everlasting life when you believe in Him (John 3:16 NKJV). I demonstrated my love for you even while you were still a sinner (Romans 5:8). I have shown my love for you by sending my matchless Son that you might live through Him. I loved you long before you loved me, I proved it by sending my son as a sacrifice to take away your sins - because I love you (1 John 4:9-10 TPT).

Love Always,
God

Reflections on Love:

"I knew we as a culture struggled to understand what love is, but I never knew our definition was in such dire need of a makeover. Our culture's definition of love is vague and vast. It is either an emotional rush or a crash, depending on the moment. It fills the heart yet also breaks it. It is the single most important resource on the planet, but humanity hasn't quite realized it yet.

"We have a culture that wants to define love before we can thoughtfully figure out what it really is. The world will always define love in a way that makes us thirst for a version that only benefits self. There is a romantic love, friendship love, love in the form of acceptance, love in the form of being admired, love that idolizes, married love, sibling love—the list goes on and on. No dictionary can give us an accurate definition or synonym for the kind of love we need. The kind of love most people chase after today is a love that is drenched in emotions and wrapped in feelings. However, that version of love will always leave you empty and searching.

"If the culture is going to be obsessed with the thought of love, we must become possessed by the truth of it."

—Micah Berteau, Pastor; *Real Love*

My Love Notes:

God is *Love*.

He is both the true reality and the true feeling of love. He did not create us like puppets to be pulled by strings. Being forced to love anyone is no love at all. God created humans with the ability to **CHOOSE** or to reject His love, so that He would be glorified by the passion of REAL LOVE.

Love: Chooses

Love Chooses Me Always!

Darla Skiles—

"Blessed be the God and Father of our Lord Jesus Christ, who has blessed us with every spiritual blessing in the heavenly places in Christ, just as He chose us in Him before the foundation of the world, that we should be holy and without blame before Him in love, having predestined us to adoption as sons by Jesus Christ to Himself, according to the good pleasure of His will, to the praise of the glory of His grace, by which He made us accepted in the Beloved."
Ephesians 1:3-6 (NKJV)

"LOVE CHOOSES."

What a different perspective to consider! Normally, I'm the kind of gal who puts my focus and attention on what "I CHOOSE." But in the last five years, I feel like I've been given the unique, God-orchestrated opportunity to see and live my life through the lens of what "Love Chooses." It's been a trip to say the least. You know, the kind of road trip you would rather sleep through or have somebody else take the wheel because you're just simply exhausted. Or like the uneasiness of NOT knowing exactly where you're going, and you're pretty sure MapQuest doesn't even REALLY know. This is where I've had to rely on what love chooses to navigate my course in life. Our ability to choose what love chooses will expose the condition of our heart. We know *who* love is. God is love. We know *what* love is. Love is patient, love is kind, love is long suffering, etc. But what does love choose?

Love Chooses ME

Say it with me: "Love chooses ME!" **To *choose* means to pick out or select someone or something as being the best of two or more alternatives.** When faced with the choice to love His people or to not love His people—no matter how lost we are, showing all our imperfections and giving Him endless reasons not to—God still chose the best of the two options. To LOVE me!

We can't even come close to comprehending the tolerance and love that God has for us. Our perspective is so small and blurred because we can't seem to look beyond our own imperfections like God can. And we definitely struggle to look beyond other people's imperfections! But God sees His beautiful creation. No matter how poorly taken care of, mistreated, used, abused, or damaged we may appear, our worth to Him is immeasurable. Our value comes from HIM, not anyone else. And He says we're priceless.

Love Chooses Sacrifice

Sometimes we think of sacrifice as if we are supposed to start "sacrificing" people from our lives. How can we be a light to others (or begin to make an impact) if we remove people from our lives? **Sacrifice is not something to be a victim of. Rather, sacrifice is something you give of yourself, or giving something of your own.** Even a small child may have to think it over for a few seconds before handing over one of her two cookies to a friend. Sacrifice is a personal loss, which can be felt on every level. It means maybe not getting my own way, even if I think it's the right way. It means giving up the "I'm right" card to save the conversation and be able to move forward. Choosing sacrifice is a sign of humility. You're daring to NOT make everything about you and instead think of another person's interests or well-being. Sacrifice is something love chooses for self—not to DO to others.

But because I love Him,
I chose to trust Him again.
I chose forgiveness.

Love Chooses Forgiveness

Forgiveness. The word that exposes everything about us. The word that draws us back into the fight. The word that, when applied, heals and restores. It puts us in a place of vulnerability to utter words of forgiveness. Who's good at that? Not me you say! I found myself in the middle of a Sunday service uttering the words "I FORGIVE YOU GOD." Yes, I said GOD. That's just the kind of relationship we have. Now you're probably thinking, *"How can you forgive God? He's perfect!"* To that I would say that your perspective of forgiveness may be too small. We can't assume forgiveness is only meant to be applied to OTHERS that have hurt you. In fact, forgiveness is for self. It's meant to heal us. And when applied, it heals the soul and restores relationships. You see there was a wedge between God and me. I put it there, not God (because yes HE IS perfect). But it was still there. I was hurt and angry at Him for what He was allowing me to walk through. I disagreed with His methods and His plan and His timing. Surely there could have been another way (little bit of my control issues coming out here). So I put a wedge between me and Him. Ummmm... correction, it was actually more like a wall between us. A really BIG one—something I'm really good at when I get hurt. Unforgiveness can rob you of so much. It can make you a slave to anger and bitterness. But I desired healing! I didn't want to be angry anymore. I desired to be   restored and in relationship again. No more stiff-arming. I applied forgiveness and yielded to His plan (even though I didn't like it because I didn't fully know what it was). <u>But because I love Him, I chose to trust Him again. I chose forgiveness.</u>

Love Chooses Always

Always. That's such a long time. That's like today, tomorrow, a week from now, next year, five years from now…. You get it.

Do I choose to love ALL the time? Nope. Sometimes for a brief moment, I believe the lie Satan whispers in my ear, telling me to hold back because I deserve better. If you've said this or even thought this, you've taken your eyes off the fullness of the garden you dwell in, and you have shifted your focus on something that will rob you of everything. Holding back love out of hurt or fear or anger will only distract you from everything GOOD that God is doing and has already given you! Emotions get in the way and, let's be honest, they TAKE OVER and we fail sometimes. Yet every second, God awards us with another opportunity to reroute and choose to love like He loves. We are given another chance to realign with HIS purpose and design, not with self or whatever new suggestion culture throws at us, but to truly repent and choose what God says is good—and choose love every time. **THE world's view of repentance says, "I WILL CHOOSE what is good for my life" (selfish and controlling). Real repentance says, "I WILL CHOOSE what GOD SAYS is good for my life."**

He sees us, He knows us, and He still passionately loves us.

And HE ALWAYS WILL.

Always is a faith-grounded word. It keeps going, doesn't stop, and when it gets distracted and knocked down by the reality of this world, it gets right back up!

ALWAYS.

Love chose Me. I choose to love.

Ask Yourself:

Have you ever felt not good enough? Not worthy enough? Not successful enough?

If your answer is yes, most of us have been right there with you. Take time to clear your focus. Look beyond your imperfections. Tell yourself: Love chooses Me!

What/Who have you sacrificed, maybe out of fear or hurt or bitterness?

God's unrivaled love desires to heal and restore all that the enemy has taken from you. Love chooses sacrifice.

What can you give of yourself in sacrifice? Time? Attention? Patience? Tolerance?

God is enough for you. You have plenty to give freely.

Where do you need to apply forgiveness so that you can experience freedom again?

Don't hold back. This is for YOU! Love chooses forgiveness.

Why is choosing forgiveness so hard? Is the vulnerability it requires too much to bear?

At times we can feel like we are putting ourselves out there in the open yet AGAIN. Exposed to hurt. But, Love...it still chooses forgiveness.

What are some examples that made you feel like you didn't want to choose love *this time*?

Remember, it's clear what God wants us to choose. Love chooses ALWAYS!

Digging Deeper:

"LOVE CHOOSES ME."
Have you ever felt alone or left out? Have you felt like you were the last woman chosen for the team, or perhaps not really ever chosen at all? We all feel that way once in a while. The truth is that God feels very differently about us than we do about ourselves. Matter of fact, He chose YOU before creation! You are loved.

Read the following verses and describe how God feels about you.

Genesis 1:27

Romans 5:8

Ephesians 1:4-6

Your value begins with the fact that you are made by the hand of the Creator in His very image. The Creator of life loves you so intensely and passionately that He allowed His own Son to die in your place before you ever repented. His plan has always been to choose YOU FIRST! Even before the creation of this world! He chose US as His own!

"LOVE CHOOSES SACRIFICE."
Read Romans 12:1 and Galatians 2:20.

What does sacrifice mean to you? What does it (or what will it) require of you?

As the Beloved, we are no longer living our lives for self, but our focus is now on choosing to live our lives for Christ in loving sacrifice.

Christ already paid the ultimate sacrifice of love by giving His life for us in death on a cross so we might experience life in Him.

Read Matthew 9:13. Fill in the blanks.

> **"I desire _____, not _____."**

So, "love chooses sacrifice" is not a mandate of bondage. The choice to live for Christ is to live loved with the gift of grace and mercy. Choosing a love life of sacrifice is choosing God's way over our own way; it is choosing spirit over flesh; it is choosing His best over our mediocre. Our living, loving sacrifice is our choosing to live in His passionate embrace and experiencing His eternal blessings.

"LOVE CHOOSES FORGIVENESS."

Read the account of Christ's crucifixion on the cross. He was betrayed, beaten, buffeted, bruised; He was spit on, shattered, shamed, and slain. Christ was put out there on display, as exposed as it gets, experiencing pain at its greatest level. (On a scale from 1 to 10, I will call that a 110.) It is probably safe to say that most of us, or none of us, have ever come close to experiencing what our Lord experienced. Yet in His greatest pain and rejection, He chooses another act of love, a deep compassionate act of love.

According to Luke 23:34, what does Jesus choose?

According to Colossians 3:13, what must our love for one another choose?

What does that kind of forgiveness look like for you on a daily basis?

"LOVE CHOOSES ALWAYS."

According to today's devotion, repentance is viewed how? Fill in the blanks.

The world's view says, "I WILL CHOOSE _____ ___ _____ _____ _____ _____."

Real repentance says, "I WILL CHOOSE _____ _____ _____ ___ _____ _____ _____ _____."

Have you uttered the words, "I deserve better; I'm not doing this again" or "This is it!"? Both are very absolute statements that will cut off any opportunity to extend love to people in your life. Today, tomorrow, a week from now, next year, five years from now...you get it. Is it easy? NO. But "we can do all things through Christ who strengthens us" (Phil. 4:13). Don't pass up the opportunity to allow God to stretch YOU, grow YOU, and help you become your best YOU.

How much emphasis does the Bible put on "love choosing always" or choosing to love others? Is it an option or a commandment? Read the following Scriptures and share your thoughts.

Mark 12:30-31
"And you shall love the Lord your God with all your heart and with all your soul and with all your mind and with all your strength. The second is this: 'You shall love your neighbor as yourself.' There is no other commandment greater than these." (ESV)

According to Mark 12:28-31, Is choosing to love always an option or a commandment?

How, and whom, should we love always according to this Scripture?

John 15:12
"This is my commandment, that you love one another as I have loved you." (ESV)

According to Jesus, in John 15:12, Is choosing to love always an option or a commandment?

How are we to love?

To God's Daughter,

_____
(insert your name)

You may not have chosen me, but **I have chosen you**. I have <u>chosen</u> you to bear fruit. I have <u>chosen</u> you so you may be given whatever you ask the   Father for in My Name (John 15:16 NKJV). You have been <u>chosen</u> to be joined with the Father before the foundations of the earth were laid. You have been ordained. You are seen by Him with an unstained innocence (Ephesians 1:4 TPT) and called His child because of the love He has lavished on you (1 John 3:1 NIV).

Love Always,
Jesus

Personal Application:

Choose God Every Day. Choosing to love God and make Him first (with all your heart, soul, mind, and strength) empowers you to love others even on their worst days. Remember, God's love chooses YOU on your worst days too.

Prayer Activation:

Dear God,

Thank you for actively and passionately choosing love. Help me to walk in the confidence of knowing that YOU CHOSE ME so that I can choose to love others. And when there is hurt in the innermost cracks of my wounded heart, help me choose forgiveness for myself and others, so that my healing process continues. And when I feel like I have no love left to give, remind me to make time to get alone with You to be refreshed and strengthened to love another day. Holy Spirit, be my guide while I try to navigate through this life, choosing what Love Chooses. Always.
Amen.

Looking for great WORSHIP SONGS?
For a playlist of beautiful songs to prepare your heart and create an atmosphere of worship...
See Appendix pages 159-161

My Love Notes:

Love: Restores
From the Ashes of Brokenness!

Devorah Robinson–

*"God, your God, will restore everything you lost; He'll have
compassion on you; He'll come back and pick up the pieces
from all the places where you were scattered."*
Deuteronomy 30:3 (MSG)

Facing the brokenness in our lives is never easy. The thought of acknowledging our pain can feel extremely uncomfortable and overwhelming. When our suffering is left unaddressed, the effects can be damaging and long-lasting. As a result, we can become trapped in the prison of our anguish, believing that we can never be free. Deeply rooted pain can fracture our spirit, causing isolation, despair, and the inability to live in the freedom and fullness of God's promises. In Psalm 34:18, God tells us that He is close to the brokenhearted and saves those who are crushed in spirit. The only way we can truly be healed is through the restorative power of Jesus Christ. It is through His great sacrifice and redeeming grace that we are made whole.

For several years, I have had the honor and privilege of leading a ministry called "Women With Purpose." It is a 10-week domestic violence support group for women who have experienced the devastating effects of physical, sexual, emotional, or verbal abuse. Imagine carrying the weight of fragmented pieces of shame, guilt, unworthiness, and fear each day, year after year—your self-esteem crushed by words and actions that wound your body as well as your spirit. These courageous women attend each week because they are determined and committed to receiving their healing. As the weeks go by, their fears start to diminish, and they begin to experience a shift in their thinking by recognizing their value and their purpose in Christ. They begin to understand and experience the depth of God's unconditional love, the power in forgiveness, and the freedom that comes through restoration. John 8:36 tells us that "He who the Son sets free is free indeed!" These women find they are no longer bound to their past. Instead, they rise victoriously from the ashes of their brokenness. It is amazing to witness the manifestation of the Holy Spirit at work in such a mighty way!

Gomer—Insulated by His Love

In the book of Hosea, God demonstrates His unrelenting pursuit of a woman named Gomer. God's desire to restore Gomer is a perfect example of how much our Heavenly Father cares about the condition of our soul. He knew that Gomer was on a path of self-destruction because of her adulterous relationships with men. God understood the depth of Gomer's spiritual and emotional state. In His unrivaled compassion, God intervened by placing a hedge of thorns around Gomer so she would be surrounded by His protection and insulated by His love. God remained faithful to Gomer even in her darkest moments.

The author of Hosea compares God's devotion to Gomer to the bond of marriage.

> *"And I will betroth you to me forever, I will betroth you to Me in righteousness and in justice, in steadfast love and in mercy. I will betroth you to Me in faithfulness. And you shall know the Lord."*
> —Hosea 2:19-20 (NKJV)

We may be able to identity with Gomer's story on some level. It is a constant reminder of God's steadfast promise to mending the broken areas in our lives so that we will return to the heart of the Father.

There is power in acknowledging the brokenness in our lives because it allows us to confront those areas without denial.

God Can't Heal What We Don't Reveal

Restoration begins when we confess and identify the origin of our pain. God can't heal what we don't reveal. There is power in acknowledging the brokenness in our lives because it allows us to confront those areas without denial. The enemy knows that if we are silent, then we will remain hopeless and disconnected from God and the work He wants to do *in us* and *through us*. When the Holy Spirit begins to expose those areas that need to be healed, with His help we can press through our discomfort and reject every lie the enemy ever told us about ourselves. It is the freedom through Christ that allows us to break from the chains holding us captive so we can experience a transformation of our hearts and a renewing of our minds. Only then can we be restored by God's unmatched love and begin to see ourselves as Christ sees us: His wonderful masterpiece!

Ask Yourself:

The enemy wants to keep us from walking in the freedom that God gave us through Christ. Are you willing to put your complete trust in God and commit to the healing He has in store for you? Like David, we must ask God to reveal the broken areas in our lives.

In **Psalm 26:2**, David asked God,

"Examine me, O Lord and try me; Test my mind and my heart."

Identify some specific areas in your life that you want God to reveal and heal. Is there anything you need to surrender to believe that God's *restoring love* is meant for you?

Describe how each of these areas have kept you from moving forward to be restored?

Digging Deeper:

The enemy seems to work overtime by attempting to create fear and doubt in our spirit and in our mind. In **2 Timothy 1:7**, we are reminded that *"God has not given us a spirit of fear, but of power and of love and of a sound mind."* This means we can be assured that whatever we are facing, God is there to see us through the most difficult times.

Think about the following Scriptures and describe how you felt God's presence and love during a time when you needed Him most?

1 Peter 5:7 – *"Cast all your anxiety on him because He cares for you."*

God can hold all of your anxiety, how does that make you feel?

Psalm 46:1 – *"God is our refuge and strength, a very present help in trouble."*

God is your place of refuge, He is your strength, and His presence is always with you. Share your thoughts.

Psalm 147:3 – *"He heals the brokenhearted and binds up their wounds."*

God wants to heal your broken heart and bind up your wounds. What does that mean to you?

There are times when our situation may seem hopeless. In those moments, it is difficult to see a way out. We can be confident that through the power of God's Word, our faith is renewed, and His promises are fulfilled.

Reflect on the following Scripture and ask the Holy Spirit how it applies to your story?

Psalm 71:20: *"Though you have made me see troubles, many and bitter, you will **restore** my life again; from the depths of the earth you will again bring me up."*

God in His infinite love for us desires to mend the broken areas of our lives so that we can live life to the fullest. It is His specialty—It's what He does best!

Read and write down the following Scriptures about restoration. Explain how each Scripture relates to you.

God's Truth	Write Down the Scripture	How It Relates to Me
Isaiah 61:7		
Jeremiah 29:11		
Jeremiah 30:17		
Psalm 51:12		
1 Peter 5:10		

Personal Application:

Sharing our testimony is very important because it confirms that God is working on our behalf while bringing hope to others. **Revelation 12:11** describes it this way: *"They have conquered him by the blood of the lamb and the word of their testimony."*

Reflect on each of the following questions and think about how you can passionately share your testimony with others.

What specific areas is God restoring in you and what are some positive changes you have experienced from God's *restoring love*?

In what way has restoration changed your relationship with God?

How does sharing your testimony about restoration inspire others?

"Restoration"

Jesus' love, shown through His death, repaired (*restored*) relationship between God and all mankind.

Love Story:

Jesus told His disciples that He would allow Himself to be broken, like bread, and then healing and redemption and wholeness would be the outcome for countless mankind. I was broken by many of life's circumstances. I felt at times like my heart had been shattered on a hard ground, pulled apart. But His loving hands pointed out the beauty in the brokenness. In the depth of my sorrow, He reminded me: "Nothing can separate you from My love."

Darlene Rhodes– PCG Pastor
(An excerpt from her book– *The Miracle of the Breaking*, pg. 138-139)

God Had a plan to "*Restore*"

Even Before God Created the World, He Made a Plan to Redeem and RESTORE the World!

- <u>Love</u> is God's motive;

- relationship is His goal;

- glory is His purpose.

- And so long before the fall,

   <u>God had a plan:</u>

   ⇒ A plan to redeem His beloved from the consequences of sin,

   ⇒ A plan to **restore** our relationship with Him, and

   ⇒ A plan to be glorified every time someone freely chooses His love.

Angela Thomas– *Reedeemed*

48

His Love Gift For All

God offers His unconditional love and calls us to humble ourselves and accept His Son into our lives. In doing so we receive the free gift of our salvation and redemption. He provides complete restoration and healing for our lost and broken souls. In our humility we recognize our own insufficiency, and glorify Him for His extravagant Grace and mercy accepting eternal life through Him.

"If you declare with your mouth,
'Jesus is Lord,'
and believe in your heart that
God raised Him from the dead,
you will be saved."

Romans 10:19 (NIV)

Prayer Activation:

Heavenly Father,

Thank You for giving me "restoring love" through the gift of Your only begotten Son as my personal Savior. Jesus, I place every broken area of my life at the foot of the cross. You are the mender of my soul and because of Your unconditional love and grace, I will no longer be bound by shame or condemnation. I am free because of the great sacrifice of Your risen Son. Help me to walk each day in the purpose and promise You have destined for me. You continue to love me despite of all my mistakes. Thank You for always seeing the best in me!

In Jesus' Name, Amen!

My "Live Loved" Declaration

Write your name in all the blanks below. Then declare God's Restoring Love toward you out loud. Then pray the same declaration over your loved ones.

For God so loved _____**, that He gave**
His only Son, that if _____ **believes**
In Him _____ **will not perish but**
_____ **will have eternal life.**

John 3:16

Dear God,

You restore my soul. You lead me onto paths of righteousness for the sake of your name (Psalm 23:3 ESV). Each day you pour your unfailing love upon me. Each night I sing your songs and I pray to you because you are the One who gives me life (Psalm 42:8 NLT). I live each day with confidence knowing that there is nothing in the universe that can separate me from your unfailing love. I know your love triumphs over death, troubles of life, fallen angels and dark rulers in the heavens. Absolutely nothing can weaken your love for me (Romans 8:38 TPT). I thank you because you restore my broken heart and you bind all my hurts and wounds (Psalm 147:3).

Love Always,
Your Beloved.

_____
(insert your name)

My Love Notes:

Love: Trusts
Removing All Fear!

Kathryn Wenth—

"Trust in the Lord with all your heart; do not depend on your own understanding. Seek His will in all you do, and He will show you which path to take."
Proverbs 3:5-6 (NLT)

I don't know of a single believing woman who doesn't want to walk in the truth of this verse. As believers in Christ Jesus, we should live life from a place of seeking His will, choosing His path, and showing the world that we trust the Lord with all our heart.

When I think about trust, I ponder all the reasons why I don't trust; and those reasons stack up like bricks, creating a wall between me and the world around me. *I don't trust because that person is not trustworthy. I don't trust myself because I might fail. I don't want to hear the truth because I can't trust that I won't be hurt by it, or that it will require more of me than I have the capacity to handle.* The list goes on and on. This inability to trust keeps me lacking in faith, which sets me walking on my own path, and it drains me of the abundance that God has for me. Not trusting Him is living in a place of fear. When I choose the way of fear, I step away from His provisional trust and choose my corrupt self-protection. Where there is no trust, there is no rest!

Our church community is bursting with new babies! It's an exciting visual, which expresses God's blessing on us as a church body. I see it as a physical expression of what He's doing in the Spiritual—reproducing new beginnings through salvation and transformation. As I look at each of these bundles of delight, I'm overwhelmed by how much God trusts their parents. His love expressed to them is the gift of a baby, a life to love, disciple, and bless! Wow! God really trusts His creation. He trusts me with the life He's given me. His will for me is my utilizing His life-giving, overflowing resources of forgiveness, hope, power, authority, faith, and the list goes on into eternity! I'm wondering if He trusts us with all His Kingdom, why is it that you and I struggle to trust Him *and* each other?

Throughout my childhood, I was not raised in a believing home. There was so much fear in the atmosphere. Fear was used to keep our large family in line. At times it was toxic, and it most certainly was consistently unsettling. As an adult, this translated to second-guessing myself, comparing who I was and what I did, and striving to control other's responses and acceptance of me. This was the way, the path I followed to survive. Even after I received Jesus at the age of 20, this trench of self-protection was my go-to when fear was directing my path. This hyper vigilance set me up to take the weight of the world on my shoulders, something that I was not created to do. Many of us live from a history where fear is more familiar than trust, anger and hate more familiar than unfailing love. God sent Jesus to heal the brokenhearted!

Fear loves to counsel me using the lies of the enemy, as well as life's hurts and misunderstandings, divisively separating me from healthy community.

My capacity to trust anyone is typically shaped from my life experiences. If I trust you, I will connect, feel safe, valued, and love being with you. This builds healthy relationship and community. If I distrust you, I will be afraid to be around you because of feeling unsafe and unvalued. Fear of being harmed will keep me at a distance. Fear loves to counsel me using the lies of the enemy, as well as life's hurts and misunderstandings, divisively separating me from healthy community. The enemy's intent is to shut me down and leave me out in the cold, naked and ashamed. The truth is, His way will lead me home! I matter *and* you matter to Him and His body!

Love and trust are intended to be woven together with our faith, creating a three-chord strand that is not easily broken. If any one of those three chords are missing, it weakens the powerful bond these three share in keeping us strong and dependent on Jesus.

Ask Yourself:

Is your whole heart able to trust and rest in the Lord? What part of your heart stumbles over trusting Him completely?

Read the key verse again—Proverbs 3:5-6.
Why do I entertain "my own understanding" and "my will," often holding it above His truth and path?

Where has your trust been betrayed? How has that impacted your ability to trust today?

Which voice is louder as you walk life's journey. The Father's *or* fear? Truth or Lies?

"Please know that God has not stopped loving you. The truth is that **God still loves you** even now, and that truth is one you can <u>trust</u> in, and that can change your world."

Digging Deeper:

In my journey, I have found that parts of my thinking and believing would rather go back to the pig slop and live prodigal from the truth. Fear and my desire to be in control are the culprits here. Part of me is 100 percent engaged with His truth, especially when everything is going well; then the other part of me struggles as if I'm walking on a slick surface, barely making it along the path I'm on. My trust capacity seems very limited at times, while at other times I'm walking on water.

Our trust in God, or anyone else, is dependent on our knowing the truth. Truth and trust go hand in hand. Hmmmm, let's reflect on this for a moment.

As a believer, when someone hurts me, do I really want to know the truth in that moment? Do I want to gain understanding and work hard to stay connected to him or her? Not typically. The hurt trumps the truth. But, as we continue to hold on to that hurt, we also tend to turn away from God's passionate truth. In those times, our trusting of Him to cleanse us of the hurt, and our ability to be able to trust the person who hurt us, becomes non-existent. When trust isn't there, neither is love really. After all, if we can't trust, there will be a part of our heart that doesn't love. For "Love

Trusts." When we are unable to trust ourselves and others, often the root is that we are struggling to trust God because we have been hurt. Loving God with a whole heart and trusting Him completely can seem impossible to do in those moments.

May I suggest to you that we love and trust others to the level that we receive God's unrivaled passionate love and immeasurable trust for ourselves? When we can accept God's love, it becomes easier to trust others by way of the truth of Jesus' death and resurrection! Have you ever looked at the cross and recognized it is in the form of the letter "t"? I like to think that "t" stands for TRUST! Without trust there is no love! "LOVE TRUSTS."

To make this concept simpler to grasp, put the word "trust" in place of "love" in this verse—1 John 4:7 (NLT).

"Dear friends, let us continue to _____ one another, for _____ comes from God. Anyone who _____ is a child of God and knows God."

"If what you see in the mirror is an example of God's passion and creativity, but you hate it, how can you really trust Him with your life?

REMEMBER: Everything good comes from above! Trust is good and comes from above. When we trust the Lord, we choose to remain in His love—to remain in Him. Remember in order to trust, we need to know the truth!

Read John 12:46 (NLT).
"I have come as a light to shine in this dark world, so that all who put their trust in me will no longer remain in the dark."

What does trust afford us in this verse?

Where do you lack light to see and trust?

Read John 14:1 (NLT).

"Don't let your hearts be troubled. Trust in God, and trust also in me."

According to this verse, what does trusting in God and in His Son Jesus protect us from?

What is your personal trust meter set on? Jesus *or* the anxiety of life?

What is a troubled heart a sign of?

What areas of life are you living in anxiety?

Read Romans 15:13 (NLT).

"I pray that God, the source of hope, will fill you completely with joy and peace because you trust in him. Then you will overflow with confident hope through the power of the Holy Spirit."

What does trusting in God open the door to?

Do you overflow with confident hope? Why or why not?

Read Ephesians 3:17 (NLT).

"Then Christ will make his home in your hearts as you trust in him. Your roots will grow down into God's love and keep you strong."

This verse is breathtaking! The fruit of trust is being rooted in God's love.

Do you feel shaky *or* rooted? At peace *or* unstable? Write your honest thoughts about where you're at today.

Visual:

When we struggle to trust God's love, we can think of this visual. Picture yourself lying on an operating table. Jesus is standing over you preparing to do heart surgery on your body. Suddenly you see yourself reach up and take the scalpel from the hand of God and say, "This is my heart. I think I have a better idea of what needs to be done here than you do." How prideful! How dreadfully silly. What is the chance that any of us can do a better job than He can at repairing our heart trust? He knows our past, present, and future circumstances. We can trust Him with it all!

To trust God is to know Him. To know Him is to know His Word, and knowing His Word provides the truth we need to fully trust Him with our whole life.

<u>Look at the following Scriptures in Psalms (NIV) and fill in the blanks.</u>

Psalm 40:4.
"Blessed is the one who _____ in the Lord."

Who are the blessed?

Psalm 52:8.

"I trust in God's _____ love for ever and ever."

What can we trust in?

Psalm 56:11.

"In _____ I trust and I am not _____. What can _____ do to me?"

Fear is the opposite of trust.
If we trust God, then we do not have to be what?

Psalm 62:8.

"Trust in Him at _____ times."

How often should we trust Him? (Sometimes, occasionally, only when things are going our way.)

Psalm 86:2.

"Guard my life, for I am faithful to you; _____ your servant who _____ in You. You are my God."

God saves those who trust Him. Also read Isaiah 25:9.

Psalm 91:2.

"He is my _____ and _____, my God, in whom I _____."

We can trust God because He is our place of safety.

Personal Application:

On the cross below, write the words of those things you want to release to Jesus. Follow that by giving it to the Lord in trusting prayer.

"We can trust fully in God though our feelings come and go, God's love for us does not."

C.S. Lewis-

To God,

Psalm 52:8 NLT
But I am like a flourishing olive tree, anointed in the house of God. **I trust** in the unending love of God; his passion toward me is forever and ever.

Psalm 13:5 NLT
But **I trust** in your unfailing love. I will rejoice because you have rescued me.

Psalm 56:3 TPT
But in the day that I'm afraid, I lay all my fears before you and **I trust** in you with all my heart.

I am like a olive tree, thriving in your house. **I will always trust** in your unending, unfailing love (Psalm 52:8 NLT). **I will trust** and I rejoice because you have rescued me (Psalm 13:5 NLT). When I am afraid, I lay all my fears before you and **I will trust** you with my whole heart (Psalm 56:3 TPT).

Love Always,
Your Fearless
Daughter

_____
(insert your name)

Prayer Activation:

Jesus,
I come before Your throne of grace. Search me and find any part of me that is prodigal in my relationship to You. I ask you to forgive me for believing the lie that You're not trustworthy and that my fears are better at protecting me than Your love. I invite You now to come and cleanse me of my unrighteousness. Forgive me for seeking the counsel of the wicked and allowing fear and hurt to take control. I invite Your truth to teach me how to trust again. I let go of the hurts and disappointment— everything that has destroyed my trust. I choose to let You restore my trust through Your love and truth. Jesus, You are my Way, my Truth, and my Light! I surrender to Your unrivaled love.

in Jesus' name, Amen.

"Trust" =

The action of "trust" in Hebrew describes placing one's reliance and confidence in another for security and safety. We must shed self-reliance, seek divine direction, and place our total confidence in Yahweh (God) to show us the way.

First 5-

My Love Notes:

Love: Serves
Serving with a "Want-To!"

Rebecca Pickett—

*"You must each decide in your heart how much to give.
And don't give reluctantly or in response to pressure. For
God loves a person who gives cheerfully."*
2 Corinthians 9:7 (NLT)

When I think of loving service, I think of hospitality. Hospitality is the gift of making family, friends, and guests feel welcomed and looked after while they are in our care. "How can I help you? How can I serve you? How can I care for your heart and ease your pain?" The root of "hospitality" is "hospital" and reminds us of the Good Samaritan. He went out of his way to check a hurting person into the hospital. He gave his time, talent, and treasure—nobody forced him! It's as simple as loving the one in front of us today, right now. It begins with taking care of ourselves, our husbands, and our children. It can be challenging when family is moody or mouthy! But we all know a warm meal—centered on plentiful protein with friendly words—can calm even the grumpiest soul.

We have to hit the reset button every morning. Bible time, prayer time, journal time, and feeling processing time is crucial. I *want* to be a cheerful giver, but when I'm reluctant, resentful, or angry, I start to "stuff it and serve on" like Martha did. She stuffed it, she served on, and pretty soon, she exploded all over Jesus and her guests! Been there, done that!

Jesus so appreciated Mary sitting down and giving Him her focused and Passionate attention.

Often, we act like Martha, trying to hold our families and churches together. Jesus so appreciated Mary sitting down and giving Him her focused and passionate attention. I think it's a balance—little bit of Martha, little bit of Mary. I still whirl around feeding my big family, homeschooling the kids, and keeping my little planet spinning. But I've been learning to slow and stop when someone needs me: to stop and say, "I have time for you. Talk to me. Even if I can't solve your problem, I will serve you with time and attention, and I will stop to pray with you about this."

Serving in Iraq for ten years, "incarnational living" has been our ministry model (Immanuel, God with us). We live in a normal neighborhood that is accessible, and welcoming people into our space is something we do on a daily basis. (All except the day our family practices Sabbath; we're closed for business that day!) When guests come, we welcome them with water, coffee, sweets, food, or tea, and then give them our best gift of all. Focused attention. A listening ear. Every conversation sliding back into the trusty conclusion: "Let's pray together about this."

People come with many needs, and we do our best to help people, using wisdom. People won't care how much we know, until they know how much we care. I've often thought Jesus sends people just because He knows we're home, we're available. Sometimes Jesus puts us into the refugees' dreams. They come and say, "I dreamt you were speaking to me last night; your lips were moving, but what was your message?" An Iraqi pastor's wife visited me briefly. Then she told me joyfully, "I have to get home, because if I'm here, I'm not there. And I need to be there, so that, if my people need me, I will be home." She was so *cheerful* in receiving guests and parishioners into her home. I really admire a strong Christian woman who gives and serves out of a cheerful joy! She was a real example to me.

I try to stay emotionally present for my husband, kids, and guests throughout the day. I like to think of this as a gift of service. Because I care for them, I will stop my task of the moment and give them my eyes, ears, and focused attention. To cry if they're crying, to laugh if they're laughing. To try not to miss the moment. We're called to follow Jesus. To do what He did. He spent a lot of time with his disciples and friends, in conversations, in meals, walking and talking together. He refreshed himself with quiet times with God, then he gathered his disciples over meals. It's a rhythm of taking in and pouring out.

If you are giving of your time and energy to serve your family, or your friends, the church (ministry), your employer, or all of the above, it is important to know your strengths and stay in your lane. God is infinite, but we are finite. We have limits. God doesn't demand that we burn out for Him. We need to practice self-care, know our limits, and learn to say no.

After my heart is refreshed by Jesus' words, I'll be able to come back and Serve with a restored heart.

I love that Mary was sitting, listening to Jesus. Mary may have been saying, "No, Martha. You're going to have to wait a few moments. I need a Heart Break right now. After my heart is refreshed by Jesus' words, I'll be able to come back and serve with a restored heart." She set a boundary with her sister. Her sister didn't want to hear it, but Jesus defended Mary. Is it hard for you to admit, "I need a Heart Break right now!"? Jesus defends our refreshing time. "Come to me, all you who are weary and burdened, and you will find rest for your souls" (Matthew 11:28, NIV).

For healthy self-care, I check in through the day: "What am I feeling, thinking, or wanting right now?" I like to take a little time to look at my feelings and thoughts when great anxiety begins to rise. I ask myself questions to clarify the angst or anger. We women get many requests and demands through the day, and it helps to serve and give from an uncluttered heart. Grabbing coffee with a godly girlfriend helps untangle feelings and also process situations. We don't have to live life alone and isolated! It's such a God gift to hear my friend's heart and to feel heard by her too.

Ask Yourself:

In Paul's letter to the Thessalonian church, he opens with a special greeting, pointing out how thankful he is for their heart to serve others. First Thessalonians 1:3 (TPT) reads, *"For we remember before our God and Father how you put your faith into practice, how your love motivates you to serve others..."*

What does Paul say motivates them to serve?

What motivates you to serve?

Read 1 Timothy 5:10 (NLT). *"She must be well-respected by everyone because of the good she has done. Has she brought up her children well? Has she been kind to strangers and served other believers humbly? Has she helped those who are in trouble? Has she always been ready to do good?"*

These four questions asked from 1 Timothy 5:10 are quite powerful. You will find them again on the next page. I, also, suggest writing them into your prayer journal.

Ask God to speak to you from these words in 1 Timothy 5:10. (Replace the she with your own name and answer the questions. Be honest.)

- *Has she _____ brought up her children well?*

- *Has she _____ been kind to strangers and served other believers humbly?*

- *Has she _____ helped those who are in trouble?*

- *Has she _____ always been ready to do good?"*

Read Romans 12:13 (NLT). *"When God's people are in need, be ready to help them. Always be eager to practice hospitality."*

What does this verse say about the heart attitude of a giver? Reluctance or readiness?

If the Lord touches our heart about meeting a need or giving an offering, should we drag our feet, or should we quickly obey the prompting? This verse gives us some clues.

Read 1 Timothy 5:8 (NLT). *"But those who won't care for their relatives, especially those in their own household, have denied the true faith. Such people are worse than unbelievers."*

I like to check in with my husband in the morning: "Is there anything you need help with today? How can I serve you today, honey?"

Think of some practical ways to care for your own family or friends.

Digging Deeper:

Read Colossians 3:23-24 (NLT).
"Work willingly at whatever you do, as though you were working for the Lord rather than for people. Remember the Lord will give you an inheritance as your reward, and that the Master you are serving is Christ."

What is the heart attitude in this verse? Who are we working for? Who will reward us? Who is our Boss/Master?

Read Matthew 10:42. In this verse, what did Jesus say would be re-warded?

Does Jesus see when we give small things with a loving heart? Does Jesus notice big smiles, hugs, or kind words?

First Peter 4:9 (NLT) reads, *"Cheerfully share your home with those who need a meal or a place to stay."*

Bringing comfort is so important to Jesus. He told us that serving a cup of cold water in His Name was like giving water to Him. I hand out water to national visitors in my home when they first arrive. It's a throwback to desert culture: parched visitors would need a drink first of all stepping inside a home. It's *doing the small things with a big love.*

How long has it been since you've shared your home doing one or both of these things outlined in 1 Peter 4:9?

As a reminder: Fill in the blanks

"Cheerfully share your home with those who _____ _____ _____
or a _____ _____ _____**."**

Ask Jesus to bring someone to your door."

In *The Path Between Us*, Suzanne Stabile teaches how we relate, give, and receive in relationships. I suggest taking a free online enneagram test. What is your enneagram number, and how does it apply to your ability to serve others inside or outside your home? My mom is a "5" and she recently sewed 85 pillowcases and 100 doll clothes' sets for the inner-city ministry. I am a "2" and an extrovert. Sewing for days would be torture for me. But that is HER life-giving, enjoyable, and needed service of love.

List some strengths and gifts you have. What do other people talk about when they discuss your special gifts? Do they talk about your great cooking, your way with babies, or your cleaning and organizational skill?

Read the following Scriptures on leading and loving through love-serving hospitality.

Hebrews 13:1-3: How are we to love others? What are we to show them?

1 Timothy 3:1-2: What attitude do leaders need when having guests in our homes?

Titus 1:7-8: This verse talks about some qualifications for ministry. What is one qualification regarding home-based hospitality?

Read Luke 10:1-42. Jesus teaches about the giving and receiving of hospitality in Luke 10.

What can we learn about receiving hospitality in verses 5-9?

Verse 7 is a famous verse we use on the mission field. Why do we eat what's set before us?

He talks about three hospitable friends in Luke 10:30-42.
Who are they? What different aspects of hospitable service can we learn from each of them?

Friend One: Lesson One:

Friend Two: Lesson Two:

Friend Three: Lesson Three:

Personal Application:

Do you know your neighbors? Jesus did say, "Love your neighbor as your-self." It's kind of hard to do that if you've never met them!

Write down the names of your neighbors below, or in your prayer jour-nal, and begin praying for them. Ask them if they need any help. Consider inviting them over for ice cream or a simple barbecue if the Lord leads. (Your neighbor is the man and woman who lives next door, but it could also be your co-worker in the cubicle or office next to yours– with that in mind, who else may also be your neighbor?)

To my Beloved,

_____
(insert your name)

You are called to be free. Do not use your freedom to serve your flesh, but **serve others through love** (Galatians 5:13 CSB). Do not just pretend to love others, but really, truly, love them. Hate what is wrong and hold tightly to what is good. <u>Love others</u> with a genuine affection and take delight in <u>honoring others</u> (Romans 12:9-10 NLT). For this is my command, my desire, for you: **Love others deeply, as much as I have loved you** (John 15:12 TPT).

Love Always,
Jesus

Prayer Activation:

Father,
I gather with my sisters at Your throne of grace. Help us Father, to love others as You love! Give us wisdom—when to say yes and when to say no. Strengthen our bodies and minds to serve with big love! Help us to not "stuff it and serve on" like Martha. When we get frustrated, help us step away for a "Heart Break" with you like Mary did. Help us do the small things cheerfully! Father, thank you for teaching us that "Love Serves"- may we serve passionately as unto You!

In Jesus' Name, Amen

For Further Reading:

Serving Exhausted:
- *No is a Beautiful Word: Hope and Help for the Overcommitted and (Occasionally) Exhausted* by Kevin Harney.

Anger and Resentment- can be signposts of crossed boundaries:
- *Boundaries* by Dr. Henry Cloud and Dr. John Townsend.

Understanding Enneagram Personality Profiles:
- *The Road Back to You*, by Ian Cron and Suzanne Stabile
- *The Path Between Us* by Suzanne Stabile

(Suggestions made by Becky Pickett)

For some hospitality recipe ideas see pages: 162-167

My Love Notes:

Love: Waits

God is in the Waiting!

Mary Price—

"Be still, and know that I am God."
Psalm 46:10 (NLT)

With social media usage at an all-time high in today's culture, it's typical to check out your newsfeed on Facebook and see that yet another couple has gotten engaged, gotten married, announced they're expecting a baby, accepted a new job offer and are moving across the country together, etc. It's very easy to focus on what other people have and get caught up in what you don't have. I know that I have personally looked at what seems to be a perfect couple's life on Facebook and thought: *If I had a man to share my life with, everything would be so much better.*

Paul writes in Philippians 4:11-13: "For I have learned to be content whatever the circumstances. I know what it is to be in need, and I know what it is to have plenty. I have learned the secret of being content in any and every situation, whether well fed or hungry, whether living in plenty or in want. I can do all this through Him who gives me strength." **We must remember that the secret of contentment in life, whatever your circumstance, is through**

Jesus Christ. It can't be found in a man, or a job, or a hobby; only through Jesus. As a single girl in her twenties, I can honestly say that it's not easy to wait for any of these things. To quote a country song, it sometimes seems like "Everybody's Got Somebody But Me." Waiting takes patience that can only be found through Christ. During this period of my life, I have learned four valuable lessons: 1) God is where we find our identity; 2) God alone can fulfill us; 3) God is forever faithful; and 4) God is in the waiting.

We must remember that the secret of contentment in life, whatever your circumstance, is through Jesus Christ. It can't be found in a man, or a job, or a hobby; only through Jesus.

GOD is where we find our identity...

Identity: the fact of being who or what a person or thing is. Once we truly figure out that our identity, our entire being, is in Christ, we are unshaken! Being exactly who God has made us to be is our purpose. Throughout life it's easy to get caught up in different titles: "I'm so and so's wife," "I'm so and so's daughter," or "I play the piano at such and such church on Sunday morning." While these are great titles, often we look past the most important title we all carry. *Being a daughter of the King gives us our identity.* God made us all for a unique purpose and gave us all different skillsets and talents. Consider these words from 1 Peter 2:9 (NLT): "For you are a chosen people. You are royal priests, a holy nation, God's very own possession. As a result, you can show others the goodness of God, for He called you out of the darkness into His wonderful light." Then, there is this powerful passage: "You made all the delicate, inner parts of my body and knit me together in my mother's womb. I praise you because I am fearfully and wonderfully made; your works are wonderful; I know that full well" (Psalm 139:13-14, NLT). The very fibers of our being have been intricately knitted together by God! Take pride in the fact that YOU are a daughter of the King of Kings!

GOD alone can fulfill us...

In a world that is constantly evolving and changing, people are looking for something constant. They're looking for a firm foundation. Someone to come to when they feel like celebrating on the mountaintop, and someone to cry with while they're going through a valley. First Corinthians 3:11 states, "For no one can lay any foundation other than the one already laid, which is Jesus Christ." Christ is our *cornerstone*. Who better to depend on being this constant in our lives than the One who created us?

GOD is forever faithful...

Sometimes in our day-to-day lives, it is good to be reminded that God is still God. He is still on the throne. He hasn't forgotten about us and the trials we are going through. Psalm 117:2 (NLT) tells us: "For his unfailing love for us is powerful; the Lord's faithfulness endures forever. Praise the Lord!" So let us praise the Lord, whether we are on the mountaintop or in the valley. Whatever our circumstance, we can rest assured in knowing that God is righteous, He is sovereign, He is omnipresent, and He is forever faithful.

GOD is in the waiting...

No matter what you're waiting on—whether it is a new job, a long-awaited relationship, a financial blessing, a prodigal to return to the Father, or a transition in life—it is easy to be overcome with impatience and eagerness. These emotions often leave us feeling disappointed, until we reach the point where we start losing faith in whatever we are waiting on. Giving up completely may seem easier than continuing to press on. It is at that moment when our trust in God must override the fear and anxiety.

I once read that "Joseph waited 13 years, Abraham waited 25 years, the Israelites waited 40 years, Jesus waited 30 years. If you are waiting for something, God has put you in good company." Psalm 46:10 (NLT) instructs us to "Be still and know that I am God..." There is no reason to grow impatient. The Bible reassures us in numerous Scriptures that the Lord will never leave us and that we are never alone. He is walking with us every step of the way, and we can go to Him for comfort and guidance at any time.

Paul wrote, *"So let's not get tired of doing what is good. At just the right time we will reap a harvest of blessing if we don't give up"* (Galatians 6:9, NLT).

May we be strong women of God and remember that He is our identity, He alone can fulfill us, He is forever faithful, and He is in the waiting. May we never forget to praise the Lord for His goodness, grace, and mercy—no matter whether we are on the mountaintop or in the valley. May we choose to be content in whatever the circumstance. May we remember that His great love for us sometimes means that we must wait, so let's lean on Him in the waiting, knowing that He has our very best in mind.

May we lead people to Christ not only at church, but through the way we live our lives for Him each day—*even while we are waiting.*

Ask Yourself:

There were four valuable lessons learned in this chapter from the character of love while in the *Waiting*. What were they? Ask the Holy Spirit how these lessons may apply to your life?

1.

2.

3.

4.

Are there areas in your life in which you are waiting on something from the Lord? (Maybe you are waiting for a relationship, a promise, a ministry or career opportunity, a healing, or a dream to come to pass.)

What are some things you can do daily to ensure that your identity is rooted in Christ?

What are some ways that you can be sure to notice the faithfulness of God in your life?

Digging Deeper:

Throughout Paul's life, he learned that whatever the circumstance, we must be content in the Lord. Paul was arrested for his faith, and he was tested many times with trials; but he learned that as long as he kept the faith and waited on the Lord, he would be just fine.

Read through Philippians 4:4-20. List areas of encouragement that Paul gives to the church in Philippi.

You may be experiencing a season of waiting. Waiting is absolutely a part of life we all experience from time to time. The more we read the Bible, the more we definitely see we are in good company. God's Word is filled with stories of people who were in a season of waiting as well.

Think of some people in the Bible who were waiting on God? How did these people react in their circumstances?

Read Isaiah 40:31.
Finish this statement.- "They that _____ on the Lord."

What takes place as a result of our waiting on the Lord according to this verse?

Read the following Scriptures and take notes on the instructions that are given about waiting.

Psalm 27:13-14

_____
_____

Psalm 37:7

_____
_____

Micah 7:7

_____
_____

Hosea 12:6

_____

_____

James 5:7-8

_____

_____

1 Corinthians 13:4 – "Love is Patient"

_____

_____

Definition of PATIENT:

Webster's Dictionary — "Able to accept or tolerate delays (long waits), problems, or suffering without becoming annoyed, anxious, or angry."

Bible, 1 Corinthians 13:4 — Read the following different versions of this same verse.

> "Charity suffereth long" (KJV)
> "Love endures with patience" (AMP)
> "Love suffers long" (NKJV)
> "Love never gives up" (MSG)
> "Love suffereth long" (ASV)
> "Love is large and incredibly patient" (TPT)

According to these definitions of patience, how are you walking through your waiting? Are you waiting in incredibly patient love, or are you annoyed, anxious and/or angry?

Waiting is not always fun. In fact, it is almost never fun; it is hard. Often, we become impatient wondering if God is going to keep His promises.

What do you discover about God's promises from the following Scriptures?

Deuteronomy 7:9	
Joshua 21:45	
I Corinthians 15:58	

While we wish we didn't have to wait, it is in the patient wait that we are strengthened, healed, transformed, and made new. God is faithful to keep His promises and gives us newfound purposes and confidence in the wait.

Personal Application:

Identify something that you can do today to make waiting on the Lord easier?

Love Stories:

"In my wait, there were times I couldn't perceive God's love and wanted to push forward in my own way. But looking back I'm thankful to now understand we can all declare: **'God loves me too much to answer my prayers at any other time than the right time and in any other way than the right way.'**"

Lysa TerKeurst– *First 5*

I remember wondering when the promise would come to pass for me. I felt like I was in a holding pattern circling the airport but not allowed to land. I felt like I was put on a shelf not being used, and too easily forgotten. I was in a waiting period that seemed to last for way too long. Waiting is not easy. During that time I questioned my purpose and God's plans for my life. Thankfully, it was in my quiet time that God lovingly met me there and gently spoke the words, "Be patient, I have a plan. Love people like I love you!" From that time forward **I knew my purpose in the "Wait" was not to sit and sulk at what was not, but to actively and cheerfully love people**. I didn't have to have a title or position to do that, just an open heart and an open door. Today, I am so thankful for that waiting time, because it was there that I felt God's love renew my soul, and I learned my most valuable lesson– to LOVE others as God loves me.

Kimberly Ming-

"The best thing we can do while we are **waiting on our miracle** is to be a part of someone else's miracle."

Lincoln Brewster-

If you are in a time of waiting listen to the Song by Lincoln Brewster: "While I Wait."

To My Patient Daughter,

_____
(insert your name)

Psalm 27:14 NIV
Wait for the Lord; be strong and take heart and wait for the Lord.

Psalm 33:18 TPT
The eyes of the Lord are upon the weakest worshippers who love him—those who wait in hope and expectation for the strong, steady love of God.

2 Thessalonians 3:5 NLT
May the Lord lead your hearts into a full understanding and expression of the love of God and the patient endurance that comes from Christ.

<u>**Wait**</u>. Be strong; take heart and <u>wait</u> (Psalm 27:14 NIV). My eyes are on even the weakest worshippers who love me and those who <u>wait</u> in hope and expectation for my strong and steady love (Psalm 33:18 TPT). I want to lead your heart into a full understanding and expression of my love and lead you in the patient endurance that comes from Christ in your <u>waiting</u> (2 Thessalonians 3:5 NLT). Will you do that, **will you wait on me?**

Love Always,
God

Heavenly Father,
I thank You that no matter our circumstance, You are always good. I thank You that Your Word gives us all the instruction that we will ever need throughout life. I ask that You give me the patience to wait on You in all areas of my life. Show me ways that You would like to fill the voids in my life while I wait. Renew my strength, restore my soul, and refresh me as I seek You. Show me how I can use my experiences in waiting to bless others. Guide me throughout my day and highlight ways that I can be like You to those around me. Reveal Your faithfulness to me today. Thank You Lord for always being with me and loving me through the "Wait."

Amen.

My Love Notes:

Love Connects:
Never Meant to Be Alone!

Kathleen Smith—

The woman left her water jar beside the well and ran back to the village,
telling everyone, "Come and see a man who told me everything
I ever did! Could he possibly be the Messiah?"
John 4:28-29 (NLT)

John 4 tells the all-too-common story of a woman avoiding relationships in order to hide her shame and regret. It's the repeated narrative of a woman attempting to protect herself from further pain or rejection. Simultaneously, it's an account of a woman encountering a love so real that isolation couldn't last long.

The fear of being fully known and fully loved is natural. We are quick to fill our schedules to the brim and put on fake smiles to avoid the time it takes to develop a genuine relationship with others... and sometimes even God. The idea of a God that so deeply and intimately loves us seems so out of reach, and the reality of a Father God that lavishes unrelenting love on his daughters can be hard to wrap our minds around. But, ladies, it's real.

This woman in John 4 knew loneliness well. She felt the rejection of others for the choices she had made, and she knew the feeling of creating her own safety box of isolation. Her journey to the well that day was made in an effort to avoid connection with others but, little did she know, she had a Messiah waiting to love her out of the isolation in which she was lost.

In this moment, the love of Jesus broke cultural norms, met her where she was, and revealed the wonder of being fully known. There's so much beauty in a love that knows our mess but still gracefully and passionately pursues us. Jesus' love was her heart's unsatisfied need; and as she encountered her Messiah's genuine love, her first response was to free herself from facades or avoidance of others, embrace vulnerability, and regain a community.

A genuine encounter with the love of God makes even the most impossible relationships *possible*.

Friendship can be challenging. People can be messy. Vulnerability can be hard. However, the strength of godly friendships is unrivaled, and the power of someone authentically living out the love of God to those around them is unstoppable.

> *Cultivating authentic relationships is a choice. The key is staying Connected to the love of God and choosing to love others as you have been loved.*

Cultivating authentic relationships is a choice. The key is staying connected to the love of God and choosing to love others as you have been loved. Maybe it's just me, but I fail God, and I fail people sometimes...guilty as charged. However, guilt and separation for my failure have never been God's response. When I connect to His love through His Word and time in His presence, He responds with more grace and more love, refining who I am every single time. So, why is it so hard for us to reciprocate and receive that kind of love from others?

In John 15, God beckons our connection to the vine—the source of life and precursor to a fruitful life in Christ. "Remain in my love," says Jesus. However, connection with Him is not a final destination. Rather, it's like a necessary layover on the journey of living a fulfilling Christian life. You must go there before being able to fully connect with others. But if you stay only there, you will miss out on the fullness of God's love. As a communal God, who created mankind for community with Him, He has designed us with an innate need for connection.

Jesus gave His life, as the ultimate act of love, to allow us to have connection to the Father. God has chosen, forgiven, healed, renamed, redeemed, and called you. He has numbered the hairs on your head and gleamed over your existence before you were even conceived. He has desired connection with you since you were born; and in as much as He has this desire, He desires for you to benefit from connection with those He places in your life.

Ask Yourself:

The woman at the well was not even intentionally avoiding an encounter with the love of God. Rather, her circumstances had clouded the awareness of her need for the love of a Savior.

In what ways have you experienced this same feeling? What has stopped you from continuing to cultivate your relationship with God? (e.g., shame, hurt, fear, religion, feeling unworthy, your past, your circumstances, worry, your own personality)

Describe a moment when the love of God met you in an unexpected, yet needed way.

In what ways can you show the grace and love you have received to those with whom you interact?

List those relationships that you believe are God connections designed for mutual benefit. Then, identify one way you can show them the love of God throughout the next week.

Friend: How will I show them love this week:

_____   _____

_____   _____

_____   _____

_____   _____

_____   _____

Digging Deeper:

Read John 4. As you read it, you can sense the shock of the woman when Jesus, a Jewish man, spoke to her. Every odd was against an interaction occurring between these two. Culturally, Jews and Samaritans were known enemies. Then, men did not casually speak to women in such ways in public. Finally, the woman was despised by her own people for her actions and was often the target of their gossip, so how much more should Jesus have avoided her? She had every right to be shocked by Jesus' boldness and intentionality, but that's God's love—bold and intentional. In this moment, Jesus spoke *to* her, not *about* her, and it made all the difference.

What has God already spoken to you?

Today, try to experience God's love for you in your day-to-day encounters.

What does God say to you through those around you?	
What does He say to you through nature?	
What does He say to you through His faithfulness in your life?	
What does He say to you through His Word?	

John 4:39 says, *"Many Samaritans from the village believed in Jesus because the woman had said, 'He told me everything I ever did!'"*

Genuine encounters with God should create an urgency within us to bring others into the same kind of love. The woman disregarded her social status in an effort to show the love of God to her neighbors.

How has an encounter with God's love propelled you to act around others?

Read Proverbs 27:17. Throughout the Bible, there are countless stories of genuine friendship or connection between two people. In some cases, it could mean between a husband and wife. As God clearly noted, "It is not good for man to be alone" (Genesis 2:18). However, the Bible reveals the value of cultivating a relationship with others, as well. Ruth and Naomi, David and Johnathan, Jesus and the disciples are all familiar friendships. God never intended for us to do life alone.

Can you think of other biblical relationships? Share a few.

Read Proverbs 27:17. According to this proverb, we should have relationships that sharpen who we are.

Do the people that you allow to speak into your life sharpen you? How do you cultivate this kind of relationship?

Read Ephesians 2:14-16. Isolation from God and others is the enemy's primary tactic in limiting your growth and fruitfulness, and his greatest plan is division. It was separation from others that kept this woman trapped in her cycle of sin. Christ's death on the cross, as the ultimate act of love, brought reconciliation—not only with God but between each other. How we defy disunity in our world today is evidence of God's love to those around us. A faith-filled connection to one another overthrows even the deepest of prejudice.

What does this Scripture reveal about walls of prejudice, separation, and ethnic hatred?

Personal Application:

Identify people that you may struggle to connect with and ask God to give you a new revelation of his love for them.

"Together" is a really good word.
Together is what we need when we hit tough patches in life.

To my Beloved,

_____

(insert your name)

Galatians 6:2 TPT
Love empowers us to fulfill the law of the Anointed One as we carry each other's troubles.

1 John 4:7 TPT
Those who are loved by God, let His love continually pour from you to one another, because God is love. Everyone who loves is fathered by God and experiences an intimate knowledge of him.

1 Peter 4:8 TPT
Above all, constantly echo God's intense love for one another, for love will be a canopy over a multitude of sins.

Fulfill the commandments of my Anointed One and carry the troubles of others for **my love empowers you** to do so (Galatians 6:2 TPT). Let My love pour continuously onto others and, when you do this, you will experience an intimate knowledge of me (1 John 4:7 TPT). Above all else, echo my intense love for others because this love acts as a canopy over a multitude of sins (1 Peter 4:8).

Love Always,
God

Father,
You desire to show me Your love as I make time to connect with You. May this time with You be evident as I encounter others. Help me to recognize Your love and give me the faith to live out Your love for others even when it's difficult. Fill my life with life-giving friendships and allow me to bring others into connection with You.

Amen.

"The deepest level of friendship is with those whose love feeds your souls. Such a friend can speak into your life with complete freedom because you know in the depths of your being she is for you."

Kay Warren– *Sacred Privilege*

My Love Notes:

Covered for a Purpose!

Darlene Rhodes—

"Keep me as the apple of Your eye; Hide me under the shadow of Your wings."
Psalm 17:8 (NKJV)

As a young teenage girl, I will never forget the moment of overwhelming shame I felt when my father was told by my doctor that I was pregnant! Fifteen years old and very pregnant. (At the age of nine, I had been molested by a 16-year-old cousin and was still silently carrying that shame.) My father was a local pastor, so in my eyes and in the eyes of my mother, I had committed the unpardonable sin. At the news, my father took a deep breath and looked into my frightened, shameful eyes; he then reassured me by saying that he loved me and that the child I was carrying would be covered with great love. He made no demands on me or the young man I had foolishly given my body to. The unrivaled God-love that "covers a multitude of sin" was the one thing that gave me hope of true forgiveness and set me on a course to walk in my God-given purpose.

> *"The Lord your God is in the midst of you, a Mighty One, a Savior [Who saves]! He will rejoice over you with joy; He will rest [in silent satisfaction] and in His love He will be silent and make no mention [of past*

sins, or even recall them]; He will exult over you with singing."
–Zephaniah 3:17 (AMPC)

While the enemy of our soul desires to hold us back from becoming who God has intended and purposed us to become, the Lord, our Father God, rejoices over us. While the enemy seeks to keep our past before us, the Lord God makes no mention of it but instead covers it with His own blood. That is truly a love that is unrivaled!

Often, we feel like we are being held back by sin and shame, or by painful unforeseen circumstances that life may throw at us—leaving us exposed and vulnerable. One of the most exciting and challenging stories I have ever heard involved a young lady named Bethany Hamilton. Bethany was a 13-year-old girl destined for a successful surfing career when she unexpectedly lost her arm to a 14-foot tiger shark on October 31, 2003. However, the attack didn't cause this determined "Soul Surfer" to give up! Instead, it compelled her to discover her purpose in life as she overcame the loss of her arm and got back on her board just three weeks later. The unrivaled love of God toward His daughters covers us in such a way that we too can look at what the enemy determines for our defeat; and we can overcome and *get back on our board* of destiny and live life to the fullest in Him.

Yet, God's love had the audacity to Cover her.

In another story—this one from the Bible—we read that Rahab saved her family's lives by taking a risk and helping Joshua's spies (Joshua 2). Rahab was a woman with a reputation, which would seemingly disqualify her to be used by God to deliver the men Joshua had sent to scout Jericho. Yet, God's love had the *audacity* to cover her. I like the passion of Rahab when she says, "I'll help you if you will save my family, because I know God has given you this land." She was well informed and acted on her information. Don't ever let the devil tell you that you are stupid, unqualified, and/or limited to what others think of you. God has you covered in His love, and He has an important purpose for you.

We need some adrenaline—some of that *passion for our purpose*—like Rahab had flowing in us!

God's *Unrivaled Love Covers* the mess and pain, and desires to use the least likely that will dare say "yes."

Can you imagine how Esther, an orphan girl, felt when she was walking into the court of the king? Or how Mary, a former demon-possessed woman, must have felt when Jesus sent her on a mission to go tell the others that He had risen from the dead? What about Mary, the young and engaged virgin girl, who was asked to give birth to the Messiah? God's unrivaled love covers the mess and pain, and He desires to use the least likely that will dare say "yes" to Him.

God has opened so many doors of ministry for me over the years. It continues to be so wonderful to know that I am loved and covered by Him. Every time I get to teach or preach at home or overseas, I still have this resounding question in my mind: *Lord, how can this be, because I know me?* My earthly father saw past my failures and hurts and knew my potential. He encouraged me and covered me with his loving kindness.

Maybe you did not have a loving earthly father who encouraged you when you failed or took missteps in life. **Let me encourage you, that our Heavenly Father has an *unrivaled love* for you! His love covers me, and it covers you, and it sits us at His banqueting table without any mention of our inadequacies. He desires to cover each of us, no matter our past, because in His love we are complete and *more than enough*!**

To read more of Darlene's story, read her new book:
The Miracle of the Breaking– My Life, His story, A Memoir
Available on Amazon

How well do you feel like you understand that God's love covers and protects you?

Have you seemingly lost sight of your purpose in life by dwelling on your imperfections?

What failures of life have you allowed to keep you from seeing how much Father God loves you?

Are you ready and willing to get back on your "board of purpose" knowing He covers your *not enough*? If not, what is holding you back?

Digging Deeper:

From Scripture you can see that God's love is like no other. His *unrivaled passion* covers us. Our sin is forgiven and covered by Father God. We don't have to live in shame and guilt when we know we have a Father who, in spite of knowing all that we have done, has chosen to pour out His love by covering our sin with the blood of Christ. His desire is to not push us away, as does happen in some earthly relationships, but to hold us close to Him under the protection and covering of His powerful and strong wing.

God also covers us so we might fulfill our purpose to glorify His great name. If you feel you have lost your purpose or you don't know what it is, pray and ask God to reveal it to you once again.

Read the following Scriptures and list some of the many ways God's love is a covering for us.

Song of Solomon 2:4	
Psalm 5:11-12	
Psalm 17:8	
Psalm 32:1 and Psalm 85:2	
Psalm 91:4	
Proverbs 10:12	
Romans 4:7	
Jude 1:1-2	

We can be so thankful that God covers us completely, leaving nothing exposed to harm or shame, in His perfect *Love*.

Have you ever felt that among all of the bad choices and life circumstances that have come your way, you have been overwhelmed and have lost the passion of your God-given purpose (or the will to discover it and be used by God)? Hold on girlfriend, according to Scripture, even the apostle Paul was amazed that God would use him. He knew his own terrible past, his more-than-poor choices, and his current daily struggles. After Paul's conversion to Christ he was called to share the gospel and tell others about Christ. Life did not become all sunshine and roses for him though—along life's journey, Paul was faced with some mighty challenges. He was beaten, shipwrecked, left to die, bitten by a poisonous snake, cast out by his own, and imprisoned more than once! However, he overcame those challenges with God's intense love and daily covering. Through it all, God covered Paul, allowing him to continue walking steadfastly in the purpose God had set before him. As a result, Paul led thousands to become Christ followers, and he wrote approximately two-thirds of the New Testament.

Read Ephesians 3:8-9. Paul called himself the least of the least of God's people. But he knew he was covered by the love of God, and there was a purpose that only he could fulfill!

According to this Scripture, what was Paul given that contributed to his ability to fulfill the call to preach to the Gentiles?

> **Paul was covered with God's _____ .**

> **You are also covered with God's _____.**

Read Esther 4:14. Esther's childhood was filled with pain and disappointment. Both of her parents had died, and she was raised by her cousin Mordecai. She was taken against her will to the palace to become either the queen or a servant. After she had found favor with the king and became queen, she was asked by Mordecai to carry out a very hard and fearful task—to save her people, the Jews.

What was the question Mordecai asked Esther?

According to Esther 8:1-8, how did God's love cover Esther to help her fulfill the purpose for which she was intended?

How might God cover you in the midst of fearful situations, which would help you fulfill the purpose He has created for you?

Personal Application:

Write down a few examples of how God has covered you with His UNRIVALED love.

Prayer Activation:

Father,

thank You for covering me daily with Your UNRIVALED love. Your love covers me—transforming my life, filling me with Your divine purpose. Help me to lean not to my own understanding in the midst of life circumstances, but to always remember I am covered by You. I find safety and protection in the shadow of Your wings. I find freedom knowing my sin is covered by Your blood. I no longer have to live in a place of shame. Because I am covered by Your love, I stand confident as the person You have created me to be. Lord, may I be used to fulfill Your purposes.

In Jesus' Name, Amen.

To my Beloved,

_____

(insert your name)

Psalm 32:1 TPT
How happy and fulfilled are those whose rebellion has been forgiven, those whose sins are covered by blood.

Psalm 103:11-12 NLT
For his unfailing love toward those who fear him is as great as the height of the heavens above the earth. He has removed our sins as far from us as the east is from the west.

Romans 8:28 NLT
"And we know that God causes everything to work together for the good of those who love God and are called according to his purpose for them."

Your rebellion has been forgiven. **Your sins are covered** by My blood (Psalm 32:1 TPT). My unfailing love towards you who fears me is as great as the height of the heavens above the earth. I have removed your sins from you as far as the east is from the west (Psalm 103:11-12 NLT). Never forget that I will always cause everything to work together for you because you love me and are called according to my purpose (Romans 8:28 NLT).

Love Always,
God

My Love Notes:

Love: Shows Up
At the Point of Give Up!

Beverly Hylton—

"God is our refuge and strength, a very present help in trouble."
Psalm 46:1 (NKJV)

Life offers us many circumstances. We will experience times of immense joy as well as times of extreme difficulty. The good news is, in every situation we can count on the Lord to be *a very present help.* He is not removed or detached from our problems, but rather He offers us abundantly available help in every aspect of our lives.

Sometimes this will call for an exercise of faith, as *His present help* is not always immediately apparent. Recently, I have personally walked this out in my own life. My husband and I have been leading our church family and community through uncharted territory, while navigating through the shocking, unexplained disappearance of a beloved 30-year-old single mother in our congregation. We embraced Najah Ferrell at church on a Wednesday evening, and by early Friday morning she had seemingly disappeared without a trace. A loving mother of two young sons who could faithfully be counted on to show up and serve others, wherever and whenever, went missing. Hours turned into days, days turned into weeks, and weeks turned into months. How could this happen? Where are the answers? Where is justice? Where do we even begin to comfort our church family and her immediate family, bravely facing each new day? Here's what I have learned and am continuing to learn: You don't always need words. When you have more questions than answers and have run out of things to say, simply speak His name. His presence makes all the difference.

Realize that the point where you want to give up is the place where God wants to show up!

> *"For I am persuaded that neither death nor life, nor angels nor principalities nor powers, nor things present nor things to come, nor height nor depth, nor any other created thing, shall be able to separate us from the love of God, which is in Christ Jesus our Lord."*
> *—Romans 8:38-39 (NKJV)*

Nothing can separate us from the love of God. Once this truth truly grips our mind, it will shift our outlook. It will put a new calm in our spirit. It will put a new song in our heart. It will give us a new confidence concerning the future. Love showed up at creation when He breathed into our being and we became a living soul. And love (Jesus) continues to be ever present in our lives. Love has no beginning, and love has no ending. We all walk through dark hours, but God doesn't get nervous when it's dark—He simply shows up. On the darkest day of all, love showed up on the cross. Now, everything else has to climb up to it! Fear must go! Sickness can't stay! Darkness must flee!

The point where you want to give up is the place where God wants to show up!

You may be in a season of uncertainty, whether the result of a tragedy, broken relationship, health issue, or a business venture. Know this: Your season won't last forever, but God's faithfulness will. What truly marks us is not the moments but the presence of God. Allow God's presence to come and kiss the situation. Jesus will show up right in the middle of un-certainty and make things certain!

God is *with* us = omnipresence.
God is *in* us = indwelling presence.
God desires to reveal Himself *through* us = manifest presence.

Love is better defined by actions than by adverbs.

Just as love shows up on the scene of our lives, we must show up for others. When you've been broken, remember that God can utilize you for something beautiful. It's only through crushing, that fragrance is released. Carry the aroma of His presence everywhere you go. There are people all around desperately searching for someone to throw them a lifeline. Perhaps God is calling you to walk across your lawn and love on that single mom, to mentor that young lady in your church struggling with insecurity, or to just sit with the elderly mother who feels forgotten. Be intentional. Ask God to show you someone who desperately needs you. Never allow others to walk alone, simply because it may be uncomfortable. You don't have to have a grand plan or all the "seemingly" right words to say. Just show up. After all, love is better defined by actions than by adverbs.

Ask Yourself:

Recall the many times God has shown up in your life during a difficult circumstance. **How have you experienced Him to be *a very present help*?**

Since God is with us *in the midst of trouble* (Psalm 46:1), how should we respond differently than those who don't know God?

What does it look like to show up for someone else?

What distractions or hindrances fight to keep you from being present?

What specific areas are you asking God to "show up" in—personally and globally?

Digging Deeper:

Read Psalm 46:1 again. According to our devotional study, we have learned that God's love "shows up" for us. **Finish this Scripture:**

"God is our refuge and strength, a very _____ help in trouble."

Describe the ways God is present. What does that mean for you?

Omnipresence =

_____

_____

Indwelling presence =

_____

_____

Manifest presence =

_____

_____

As Christians, we strive to live out our faith with joy and maintain a positive outlook on life. Still, without question, it takes courage and stamina to face the days in which we live. Daily, we hear news of tragic events in our country and our world. The truth is, we are not exempt from problems. If God promises to show up and come to our aid _in_ times of trouble, we understand that we will invariably face difficulty and adversity.

Are you confident _or_ fearful as you look toward the future?

Do you find it unsettling to see the degree of unrest in the world right now?

Are you ever worried about your family's safety and security in such uncertain times?

Read Psalm 46:1-11.

Although adversity may be a fact of life, these verses assure us that in good times and bad, our Lord walks with us. Knowing that He is our very present help can empower us and enable us to be courageous as we face life—with all its blessings and challenges.

These verses speak of turmoil while still remembering God's sovereignty. Why is it so easy to focus on one or the other, but usually not both at the same time?

The Psalms were originally musical compositions. They provided the lyrics for inspired hymns. **Look at Psalm 46 again**. It is divided into three stanzas, each ending with the Hebrew word "Selah." Originally, this word was most likely a musical notation indicating a pause in the music for contemplation on what was just sung. You might read it, "Pause and think on that," or perhaps even, "Pause and let that sink in."

These three *Selahs* give us the structure of the psalm. Verses two and three refer to times of physical catastrophe. Verses four through seven refer to the threat of warfare. And in verses eight through eleven, when the future seems uncertain, this is how you handle that.

> Don't panic; pause.
> No need to fret and fear; pause.
> And in place of worry and anxiety, pause.

The foundation is firm. The Lord is our refuge. He has shown up as our present help in trouble.

The proof is in the promise!

Read Isaiah 41:10 and Isaiah 43:2.

According to these two Scriptures, when we are fearful and discouraged where does God say that He will be?

Is there a difference between God helping us when we are in trouble and God being with us in trouble? Why or why not?

Read 1 John 3:18.

Is there a difference between saying you'll show up for someone and showing up for someone? Why or why not?

Saying you'll be there for someone is not the same as actually *being* there for someone. Being there is being there. If we are not careful, we can very easily become self-absorbed. Just as we desire God and others to show up in our lives, we have a responsibility to reciprocate. Intimacy grows in a relationship when we are present. Since God is ever-present in us, He de- sires continual fellowship/ conversation with us.

I'm constantly challenged and inspired by the lifestyle of passionate devo- tion found in one of my mentors. The first thing every morning, she sits at her desk and writes God a love letter. She simply thanks Him for another day, praises Him for who He is, and tells Him what He means to her—all while expressing her devotion to Him. She has done this for years; wheth- er she's at home or traveling. She's left notes on countless hotel desks across the country, and I just have to believe that many have even come to know Christ as a result of finding them. Genesis 5 shares of a man who followed God with passionate devotion, as well. Enoch walked with God and lived in such close fellowship that God took him! Now that's showing up!

Read Titus 2:3-5. What does this verse advise women to practice in the way of showing up for others?

I want to tell you that the younger women in your life need you. They need your wisdom, especially the wisdom learned through your mistakes, failures, and even the tragedies of life. Remember, none of it is wasted with Him. *The good news is, we all have someone older than us and someone younger than us, so we never stop.*

"Show Up"

Don't overthink it.
Don't worry about relating. If you are a woman who loves God and His Word and are intentional in seeking to love younger women in your life, growth will happen. He'll make it happen, often in the least expected moments.

Initiate.
Assumptions are rarely correct. Don't assume that a younger woman has an older woman in her life. Also, please don't assume that you don't have what it takes. Prayerfully ask the Lord who you should reach out to, and then do it. Keep it simple. Invite them to lunch or to grab coffee. Let the Lord lead the relationship.

Be Yourself.
Most all of us value authenticity. A younger woman isn't expecting a perfect woman to disciple her. Your unique, personal story is part of a bigger narrative. She just desires someone real to show up, to share, and to be present. God is waiting to write the best chapters—stay in the story!

Personal Application:

How are you purposeful in showing up to meet with God?

Has any area become simply routine or a duty? If so, what can you do to rekindle your passion? (Search and write down Scripture texts that inspire you.)

What would you write in a letter to "your younger self" about who you have found God to be, what He means to you today, and the situations where His presence made all the difference?

Be careful of those willing to **show up** to criticize, warn & give you worst case scenarios. They're less invested in you, and more invested in their own opinion.

– Havilah Cunnington

To my Brave Daughter. _____
                                                    (insert your name)

In times of trouble, you can have the confidence to approach me, for I hear you when you ask anything according to my will (1 John 5:14 NIV). In times of chaos, be strong and courageous. Do not be afraid or panic. Know that I personally go ahead of you and that I will never fail or abandon you (Deuteronomy 31:6 NLT). Have no fear because I, your Heavenly Father, am for you, so what can mere people do to you (Psalm 118:6 NLT)?

Love Always,
God

God's Love not only **SHOWS UP**-
It never leaves, it never forsakes,
And will never separate from us.

Romans 8:38-39

Prayer Activation:

Father,

Thank you for always showing up, and for being a very present help to me at all times. Thank you for never leaving or forsaking me. Your presence is life and strength to me. I commit myself unreservedly to Your purpose. Help me to be intentionally aware of those around me, showing up for them with a new level of sincerity and courage daily.

Amen.

My Love Notes:

Love: Lifts
Up and Out of the Pit!

Angela Foster—

*"He lifted me out of the pit of despair, out of the mud and the mire.
He set my feet on solid ground and steadied me as I walked along."*
Psalm 40:2 (NLT)

Love Lifted Me

You may be familiar with a popular hymn from long ago that echoed the words, "Love Lifted Me." In 1912, James Rowe wrote the lyrics to this hymn and, fittingly, these three words became the song's reassuring title.

> *"Love lifted me! Love lifted me! When nothing else could help, love lifted me! I was sinking deep in sin, far from the peaceful shore, very deeply stained within, sinking to rise no more. But the Master of the sea, heard my despairing cry, from the waters lifted me, no safe am I. Love lifted me! Love lifted me! When nothing else could help, love lifted me!"*

Rowe wanted to convey the idea that we can sink into sin just like the apostle

Peter began to sink into the Sea of Galilee when Christ called him out to walk on the water. But love reached down and lifted him. A few years ago, I too found myself sinking into waters of discouragement and self-judgment. I needed the Lord to lift me up and out, and He did.

I have been a Christian woman for all my adult life, and I am currently an active- duty Army chaplain wife. My involvement in ministry spans more than 23 years. With my husband, I've had the great privilege and opportunity to travel across the United States and the world. We have ministered to many people and served with some amazing women of God—women I look up to and admire. Many times, however, I compared myself to these strong, well-spoken, and educated women. I even caught myself becoming discouraged and wishing I could speak the way they did. They had a gift that seemed to come naturally, and they spoke with such clarity and conviction. And if it wasn't their speaking ability, I wished I could come up with crafty ideas and execute a program like these women did so well. But those gifts were not what God had blessed me with, so I found myself "far from the peaceful shore" as the song lyrics go.

She simply revealed the love of God to me and *lifted me up* through her words of encouragement.

The love of God shining through one of these dear women finally lifted me up and out of the muck I was in. It happened after we moved to Italy in 2015. While talking to a friend one day, I shared my passion to mentor and encourage women. I said to her, "I wish I was more like you and could speak and teach like you do. I wish I could impact women like you do." She gently spoke into my life that day. She said, "Angela, God didn't create you to be like me. He created you to be you and He has given you gifts, talents, and your own personality to reach others." She told me that I needed to embrace how God created me and to impact others for His Kingdom.

This insightful woman didn't try to tell me what my God-given gifts were or what I should pursue, she simply revealed the love of God to me and lifted me up through her words of encouragement. Soon after, I had the opportunity to start a mentorship program with some young military wives. For the next year and a half, I was able to walk beside (and do life with) a group of women whose greatest passionate desire was to become the women God created them to be.

As I loved on these women, and rejoiced with them as they discovered God's plan in their own lives, I found that it not only encouraged and lifted them up, but it encouraged and lifted me up too. You see, I didn't have to be a dynamic speaker or have a bigger-than-life personality to love and encourage women. God was using me just like He made me. I still learn from, grow with, and admire the women who have all those other gifts; but now I understand I can be different and that's absolutely fantastic with God! I was lifted up and out of the pit of despair. Because a woman of God shared God's love with me and was willing to speak truth, I became free to be the ME God created me to be.

As women it is critical for us to understand that God is passionately crazy about us. We must embrace His love and who He created us to be. In 1 Thessalonians 5:11 (NLT), Scripture says, "So, encourage each other and build each other up just as you are already doing." I believe God wants us to help each other by lovingly encouraging each other to operate in our own gifts and talents—not our neighbor's. When we stop trying to be who we are not and embrace *who we are in Christ*, we find freedom and joy.

We can be the love of God that lifts someone else out of their miry clay. As the end of the song declares, "Love so mighty and so true, merits my soul's best songs; faithful, loving service too, to Him belongs. Love lifted me!"

Who is like the Lord our God, who is seated on high... He raises the poor from the dust and lifts *the needy from the ash heap, to make them sit with princes, with the princes of His people.*

Ask Yourself:

When you talk negatively about yourself, it holds you back from all God has in store for you. How do you talk to yourself?

Are you able to be happy for the achievements of other women, or do you find that you are self-comparing, jealous, or even bitter?

Does comparing yourself to others keep you from doing or being the person God has created you to be?

What are your strengths, personality traits, and gifts? How can you use them for ministry?

How can our words and actions affect those that are serving beside us?

Digging Deeper:

When we find ourselves in a pit of despair, the first thing we often do is run to a friend for encouragement. Usually, we choose one whom we know will empathize and agree with our side of the story. Other times, we may choose isolation, shopping, eating (way too much), binge watching Netflix; or we might even choose to take a pill or drink to forget about the circumstance.

What help are these things when we need to be lifted up and out of a dark place?

Read Psalm 40:2 (NLT).
"He lifted me out of the pit of despair, out of the mud and the mire. He set my feet on solid ground and steadied me as I walked along."

When David found himself in a pit of despair, where is the first place he went for help?

Why should we look to God's love to lift us up before we do anything else?

Read Matthew 14:22-33. Jesus walked on the water, and Peter called out to him, "Lord, if that's you, tell me to come on the water." But when Peter began to walk on the water, he took his eyes off Jesus, focusing on the stormy water. He was filled with fear and doubt and began to sink. *Down, down, down.* Jesus immediately reached out to Peter and lifted him up and put him in the boat. Jesus used this situation as a learning experience for Peter to trust Him. When we focus on God's love, trusting and believing in Him, then we can (spiritually) walk on water.

What happens when we take our eyes off of Jesus and focus on our-selves—on our lack, on our problem, on our despairing pit?

When we feel like we are drowning, what happens when we look back to Jesus?

There are times when it seems like we are going through one despairing pit after another. King David often felt that way. Jonah felt that way. Moses felt that way too. Nevertheless, God always walked them through their pits and the mire and lifted them to a place of greater trust, influence, and authority.

Read the story of Joseph (Genesis 37, 39-47). Joseph was literally put in a pit by his brothers. This was an obvious place of hurt and despair. What Joseph didn't know was that he would be lifted back up out of that pit, only to find himself sold in an Egyptian slave trade. That became another pit of despair, but then Joseph was purchased by one of the pharaoh's officials and lifted up to a place of leadership—only to be faultily accused by the pharaoh's wife and thrown into prison. While in that pit, he was lifted up to a place of favor by the prison warden, yet he was betrayed and forgotten by friends. Joseph was finally lifted out of the pit, out of his prison. God lifted him up to become the greatest influence (just under the pharaoh) in all of Egypt and all of the surrounding nations, ultimately bringing salvation to the nations and to those who threw him into his first pit.

Do you believe that God lifts us up through our "pits" to set us in a greater place of trust, influence, and authority?

Read the following Scriptures. Write them out in your own words, making them personal to you. Go back and circle how God's love lifts us up.

Psalm 71:20	
Psalm 97	
Psalm 113: 7-8	
Psalm 146:8	
Isaiah 63:8-9	
I Peter 5:6	
James 4:10	

Read 1 Thessalonians 5:11.

"Therefore, encourage one another and build each other up..."

What was the apostle Paul's advice to the Christ followers?

If you look further at the passage (verses 9-11), you will see that Paul, the author of the letter to the Thessalonians, was encouraging the Christ followers. He told them that God didn't come to appoint us to suffer wrath but to receive the gift of salvation through our Lord Jesus Christ. His "unrivaled passion" was so great that He died for us. He provided the ultimate form of lifting us out of our pit: redemption. He did that so, whether we find ourselves dead or alive (or I might say, in a place of despair or joy), we can choose Him and have life! A life that we can live with Him.

He went on to say, "Therefore...," meaning that because we have life in Christ, NOW we can share that life with others. We can encourage and lift others up as Christ has come to lift us up.

How has Christ lifted you?

In that same way, you have been gifted to lift up others. What Christ has done for you becomes your love-lifting story.

We are living in such a self-centered world, often filled with negativity and critical spirits. Instead of spending time tearing others down (whether in our own minds, in person, or behind their backs), it would be much better for us to spend our energy lifting one another up. There is blessing in love-lifting! So, let's focus on building each other up (lifting each other up), following Paul's practical advice in 1 Thessalonians.

Read Luke 5:17-26. This is a beautiful, historical story of faithful friends who lifted a paralyzed man from his mat and carried him to Jesus. Keep in mind, they didn't just lift him up by offering encouragement, and they didn't just lift him up by physically picking him up; they lifted him up by offering him Jesus!

What is the first thing that we should offer to our friends in their moments of despair?

How did lifting him up to Jesus change the paralyzed man's life forever?

What effect did it have on those who were in the room?

How do you think it may have affected those who had known the paralyzed man for years?

How do you think it affected the lives of the friends who took him to Jesus?

When we lift someone up instead of walking past them (or even worse, tearing them down), the effects of that one act of "love-lifting" can be far reaching. Likewise, instead of tearing ourselves down with words like "I'm not good enough, capable enough, or talented enough," we should self-apply the same love-lifting philosophy.

Read the following verses and reflect on some practical ways Scripture shares how we can lift others up.

SCRIPTURAL VERSE:	LIFT OTHERS UP:
1 Corinthians 13:4-7	
Ephesians 4:2	
1 Thessalonians 5:11	
Hebrews 10:23-25	
Ephesians 4:29	
Acts 20:32	

To God,

You are a God of passionate love. I know you will meet with me and empower me to rise in triumphant victory (Psalm 59:10 TPT). You open the eyes of the blind. **You lift** those who are weighed down. You love the godly (Psalm 146:8 NLT). **You have lifted me** out of the slimy pit, out of the mud and mire, and set me on a rock and gave me a firm place to stand (Psalm 40:2 NIV). I praise you and thank you for your love and all that it has done, is doing, and will do in my life.

Love Always,
Your Beloved

_____
(insert your name)

Personal Application:

In what ways can you show God's love and lift others out of their pit of despair? In other words, how can you be a LOVE-lifter?

Prayer Activation:

Lord,
Thank You for lifting me up and out of my pit of despair. Thank You for creating within me all the gifts and talents that I need to be exactly who You created me to be. Help me to not compare myself to others but to live fully in You, just as you have made me to be. Help me to encourage and lift up other women as they do what You have called and prepared them to do for Your Kingdom. Help me to build up and not to tear down; to encourage and not discourage; to speak truth in love; and to speak life. May I walk in Your "unrivaled love" and be passionate about being a love-lifter!

Amen.

My Love Notes:

"**God's love** is redemptive, relentless, and unconditional. As each of us becomes rooted in God's extravagant love, we'll experience a freedom and a confidence that empowers us to become who we were created to be."

-John Bevere

Love: Grows
A Multiplied Harvest!

Julie Lester—

"All over the world this gospel is bearing fruit and growing, just as it has been doing among you since the day you heard it and understood God's grace in all its truth...We pray...that you may please him in every way: bearing fruit in every good work, growing in the knowledge of God, being strengthened with all power according to his glorious might...and joyfully giving thanks to the Father." Colossians 1:6, 10-12 (NIV)

Love Knows No Bounds

Every morning for the past year, my son Josiah comes out and greets his dad and me with his special grin. He lifts his head, juts his chin out, and stands *oh so tall* in order to *show* us how much he has grown. In a couple of years, I will miss the routine of his sharing this progress with us. Even better than observing the changes of Josiah's physical stature is recognizing the evidence of spiritual growth in our son. What great joy for a parent to see some of the spiritual lessons of life take root and produce actual fruit! What we sometimes forget, though, is that in the same way we are facilitating and observing the progression of our children as they grow up; God, our heavenly

Father, is doing the same for *us*! Because we love our children, we want them to grow in all kinds of amazing ways. Because God loves *us* so much, HE wants us to grow, only on a bigger more passionately intentional scale! If only we could recognize our progress, over time, through all the ways and in all the seasons God has provided opportunities for our own spiritual growth.

God's intention is *always* growth.
God's plan for intentional growth for His children is not just the simple, single-faceted, temporary variety. Nope. He is all about expansion. That is why in Genesis 1, God plants seed-bearing plants and trees (11-12); commands creatures to "be fruitful and increase in number..." (22); and also commissions mankind to "be fruitful and increase in number; fill the earth..." (28). He is the *source* (who is also the *catalyst*) for more to come, and He has bigger, grander things on His mind. In Mark Batterson's book *Whisper*, he proposes that during creation when God commanded, **"Let there be...,"** the impact of His words are still in effect today! His Word cannot be contained but instead manifests exponential results!

God's plan for "*love-growth*" is multifaceted.

God's plan for love-growth is multifaceted. It often operates on the intricate, personal, inside-out level. But it *also* swells to the far-reaching, interpersonal, body-working-together kind of macro level in order to impact the world on a larger scale. The precision of personal heart work is His specialty. God is all about the nurturing of the planted seed, but we also see how He takes something that seems small and insignificant and demonstrates what amazing things are possible in His hands! He wants to produce through us many more times that which was sown (Matthew 13:23). In God's love, He sees growth through from start to finish, but sowing the seed which produces a plant is merely the beginning. He wants to distribute and multiply that harvest so *as many as possible* can partake!

God's intention is always growth *and* inclusion.
In other words, God is continually and intentionally involving all of us in His

business. And what a business it is! It is not merely the temporal, mediocre, mundane realm—it swells beyond our physical borders to the eternal, powerful, His-Kingdom-Come kind. God commissioned our involvement in His story right from the beginning in the garden. Daily, He gives us resources that are both readily available and untapped. He wants us to explore, work, invest and grow.

When Christ, God the Son, enters the human scene, He does things the way He has always done them. He calls people to join Him in what He is doing. That is why Jesus called and equipped His disciples; and that is why, right before He left them, He gave a new command that reflected His initial command in Genesis—but with further reaching, eternal implications: "Go into all the world and preach the good news to all creation" (Mark 16:15). His first mandate (in the garden) had physical, temporal capacities. The second had spiritual, eternal implications. Both commissions include us. Both called for increase. But the latter brings us back into conformity with His will: To tell the world that God has made a way, through Christ, to bring us back to where we have always belonged—in relationship with our Creator.

God's intention is always growth, inclusion *and*, ultimately, praise.
That is the whole point! We were created to grow up to become productive, relational members in God's family, but He also created us to bring Him glory! It is important that we not only pour out our lives in service to God, but that we continue to grow passionately in love with Him, giving Him all the praise. We can work hard to grow in knowledge and wisdom, grow in wealth and resources, and do it all with the purpose of increasing the harvest. But we must personally continue to grow passionately in love with God daily, pouring out our humble worship and adoration to the One who poured Himself out for us.

With all that we put our hands, heads, and hearts to do, may it be done with Christ always in our view. Let our eyes be focused on Him and our lives perpetually point toward Him in all that we do. Jesus emphasizes this: "Let your light shine before men, that they may see your good deeds and praise your Father in heaven" (Matthew 5:16). God lovingly includes us in His work. Now let His love passionately grow and multiply a harvest through each of us to the world, and may we not forget that it's ALL about Him!

Ask Yourself:

God's love means that He intentionally allows certain circumstances in our lives to facilitate our spiritual growth. Some of these things prove to be physically, emotionally, and spiritually challenging. If you are like me, you enjoy the comfort and safety of familiar surroundings. Often, we fear the circumstances that promote the most spiritual growth because they entail things that are bigger and more difficult to deal with under our own power. This can be scary. After all, we would rather feel like we are in control of our own situations than entrust ourselves to God. When we are willing to surrender something of ourselves to God, He often shows us that He can do something bigger and better with it than we ever could by holding on so tightly.

Read John 12:23-26.

What do the words "Unless a kernel of wheat...dies" mean to you?

Is there an area of your heart that you are holding on tight to, not willing to surrender it into the Lord's hands?

What are some things He promises us if we are willing to die to ourselves?

A life routine can be easy to maintain. Day after day, month after month, year after year, but God wants to invade the neat (or messy) little space we have created for ourselves. As an example: When you leave a tomato plant in a little pot, it will only grow to a certain point. Its roots will become confined and bound, and its growth will stagnate. The same can happen with certain kinds of turtles and fish. We once had a turtle that remained quite small. We thought that was just its normal size. When we moved, the turtle went to a new home and was placed in a larger environment. Bet you don't know what happened next. Yep, that tiny turtle grew and grew! Who knew?

Well, God, the master designer of all things that grow and expand and multiply, created you and me and His Body to grow—inside and outside! Paul writes that "the kingdom of God is not a matter of talk but of power" (1 Corinthians 4:20). It takes God's energy or power, running through you, to grow beyond the confines of your comfortable little space—the one you have been so carefully maintaining. He would like access to your soil (maybe even to transplant you into a bigger container) to ensure your roots can stretch out and your branches can grow a little longer so, ultimately, you can produce even more fruit.

Are you willing to allow God access to your internal *pot of soil*? What area(s) do you believe the Lord wants you to grow?

Is there anything binding the roots that need room to sink down into Him, which may be hindering the kind of growth in you that will produce an abundance of healthy fruit?

> "No one but you is responsible for your spiritual life. No one can force you to grow in your faith. No one but you can **grow** a deep soul inside of you."
>
> —Kay Warren, *Sacred Privilege*

Digging Deeper:

God includes us in His work! But why should He go and do something like that? We often mess things up. Am I right? Why would a perfect God who does everything exactly the right way choose to use *us*? I believe it's all for Him, for His pleasure and His glory, and...because He *loves* us too. His love has always been relational and inclusive. He wants YOU! He wants YOU to grow, *and* He wants to include YOU in the family business. All the way and every day!

Is there something you have been through or done that makes you feel inadequate or not good enough for God to use you?

One of my favorite historical stories is the famous "Feeding of the 5000." This true event is recorded in all four gospels: Matthew 14:15-21, Mark 6:30-44, Luke 9:10-17, and John 6:1-14. I suggest you read all of them, as each contains certain details you would miss if you only looked at one. Also, read them in context of the whole chapter to gain a clearer picture of the *behind-the-scenes* setting for the circumstances of the day. Significant things are happening right before and right after this important miracle. I would especially look at the whole of John 6, because the author specifically unpacks the event and its deeper significance. Try to put yourself in the sandals of the different people who are portrayed in this story. There are the disciples. There is a massive crowd. There is a boy. And there is Jesus.

Read Matthew 14, Mark 6, Luke 9, and especially John 6.

What was going on with both Jesus and the disciples *before* this particular miracle?

What was the intention of Jesus, right before all the people started showing up?

Set the unfolding scene. What was going on and who was around? What was Jesus' response to the crowd? What did the disciples start noticing?

How did Jesus respond to the disciples? (What solution did they come up with? In what ways did Jesus involve them in this miracle? Who else was involved?)

Did you notice how long the day was—stretching on and on? What are some of the amazing miracles the disciples would have missed out on if Jesus had called it a day at different points throughout these chapters?

Did you ever take a hike or drive only to hear someone say repeatedly, "Let's just go around the next bend"? And you keep doing that again and again. Jesus seems to do that at this particular time. This day seems to be the day that never ends! In fact, if you noticed, that one day seems to blend right into the next, with very little recovery room. It makes me tired just thinking about it! But one of the themes evident throughout this eventful day is the way Jesus was stretching the disciples. He wanted their faith to grow. He wanted to take them to a place beyond themselves—a place where the impossible would happen outside the normal boundaries of the physical world. He wanted to show them that even when there seems to be a great lack of resources, a lack of time, and they're all running on fumes with little left to give, He still plans to use them in a significant way. But there are two caveats: He gets to show up *big time*, and He gets to talk about who He is. In the process, growth and expansion will be MULTI-PLIED for ALL involved!

Read John 6:22-40. John includes a conversation that culminates the whole point of the kind of miracle Jesus performed that day.

What "I AM" declaration does Jesus proclaim in verse 35? How is this significant?

God lovingly includes us in His work, but He also provides ALL that we need to accomplish what He asked. We NEED Him, and He loves giving to us in abundance those things we need. In fact, He gave ALL of Himself for us! He continues to give Himself, but He beckons us to partake wholly in what He has to offer. As we fill up with Him, He will help us grow healthy and strong and enable us to have the energy to go a little further—as far as He wants to take us.

What areas do you feel weak or insufficient in that you know without Jesus growing something bigger within you will prevent you from accomplishing something He's asked of you?

We can feel overcome with the amount of pouring out that life takes on us at times. Often, we feel weak, tired, and depleted in every form—mentally, physically, and spiritually. What we have feels like it cannot sustain us—it is insufficient! It's true that left to our own devices, strength, and power, we are weak indeed. Here we are with only two wee fish left in our hands, and we really are not even sure about one of them.

What words of encouragement would you give to a sister who may feel similar? What gleanings can you share with her from the stories you just read in Scripture about how Jesus can expand and grow what we have? What does Paul remind us in 2 Corinthians 1:8-11 about why God allows difficult situations that are bigger than ourselves?

Personal Application:

We don't want to end our time together without remembering to practice the most important aspect of our relationship with God. We might have an extremely high production rate, which seems to point to great amounts of growth coupled with abundant harvests; but if we lose sight of our First Love then we have lost much indeed. He has been so intentional to include us and provide opportunities for growth. Let's take some time to grow that love and passion through our humble worship to Him.

Write down some praises to God. Include some specific attributes that you are thankful He displays in your life and in the world around you.

Write down a way you know He has grown you this past year. Thank Him for providing the experience and for being with you through it.

To my Beloved,

_____
(insert your name)

My hope is that the love in your heart will overflow more and more and that you will continue growing in knowledge and understanding (Philippians 1:9 NLT). Grow, in every way, more and more like Christ, who is the head of his body, the church, and speak truth in love (Ephesians 4:15 NLT). As you are growing, look for me whole-heartedly, and when you look for me, you will find me (Jeremiah 29:13 NLT).

Love Always,
God

Reflections on Love:

Growing in God's Love-

"God won't stop reminding you He specializes in multiplying little into much. He'll continue to pour His sufficiency into you, giving you the strength, energy, and passion you need to fulfill His calling. He will whisper to you everyday that you matter because He chose you, He loves you, and you belong to Him. You, my sister, are ready for anything and equal to anything through the Resurrection power of Christ Jesus."

- Kay Warren

Prayer Activation:

Father,

I thank You for loving me so much that Your desire has never been for me to remain stagnant and unproductive, but instead You are a God of fruitfulness and multiplied harvest. Thank You for including me in Your work, providing the resources and strength I need to accomplish what You have intentionally commissioned me to do. Thank You for taking my offerings (sometimes the little I have left) and multiplying the effect of them in ways that only You can. You are my source, and You are the provider of my growth and exponential increase. May You be forever glorified in my life, and may the world see You through me!

Amen!

My Love Notes:

Love: Extends
Feed My Sheep!

Micah Yursik—

When they had finished eating, Jesus said to Simon Peter,
"Simon son of John, do you love me more than these?"
"Yes, Lord," he said, "you know that I love you."
Jesus said, "Feed my lambs."
Again, Jesus said, "Simon son of John, do you love me?"
He answered, "Yes, Lord, you know that I love you."
Jesus said, "Take care of my sheep."
The third time he said to him, "Simon son of John, do you love me?"
Peter was hurt because Jesus asked him the third time, "Do you love me?"
He said, "Lord, you know all things; you know that I love you."
Jesus said, "Feed my sheep."
John 21:15-17 (NIV)

Jesus calls all of us to live a life that is so touched and moved by His love toward us that it pours out into others as a natural overflow. When Simon Peter finally received the revelation of God's unrivaled love toward him, and he came to the understanding of God's deep desire to be in true relationship with him, then the Lord's immediate response was to call Peter to make an action step to "Feed my sheep." When we have experienced the true love of Jesus through heart change, the immediate call for each of us becomes to go and extend that love to others. A God kind of true love invokes action! His love is so grand and forward that it requires a response! His love induces passion, not passivity. The Book of Revelation says that Jesus is our Bridegroom husband. Our husband Jesus is not passive; He has put Himself all the way out there with an extravagant display of His love for us, and we must respond! In this key passage of Scripture from John 21, Jesus is telling Peter that it is time for him to respond to the love He had poured out for him on the cross.

Peter's Problem

Many of us can probably identify with Peter. The problem Peter had was that he was notoriously ruled by his emotions. He was what we would call an "external processor." In other words, he was always the first person to say what everyone was thinking, and it usually got him in trouble. He said and did some seriously cringe-worthy things—like rebuking Jesus for going to the cross or blurting out something that made no sense during the transfiguration. He even started a fight trying to protect Jesus, which ended with someone's ear getting cut off! With that said, he was also the first person to stand up in displays of raw passion and faith—like when Jesus called out to the disciples on the water, and Peter was the only one who got out of the boat and walked on water to meet Him! So, when we start to think that our key passage of Scripture might sound as if Jesus was being pretty harsh toward Peter, we have to remember they had quite the history; and Jesus knew exactly what He was doing!

Peter's emotion-driven nature had gotten him in some trouble not long before this moment when Jesus confronted him with the question "Do you love Me?". Peter was a devout Jewish man who deeply understood the promises concerning the Messiah. Up to this point, he had walked intimately with Jesus for years. He knew Him well and dedicated his life to the belief that He was the promised Savior King that Israel had been waiting for. But, after Jesus told him and the rest of the disciples that He must be crucified and resurrected on the third day to fulfill His plan of salvation (Matt. 16:21), things started to get a little shady for Peter. When it came time for Jesus to save the world and go to the cross, Peter got so discouraged by how grim things were looking for Him, he actually publicly denied ever having been associated with Jesus. Not just once—he denied him three separate times! Ouch! Ouch!! OUCH!!!

Confrontational Moments

Now let's fast-forward to this confrontational moment between Jesus and Peter. This was the third time Jesus had appeared to His disciples since His resurrection. They were enjoying a glorious reunion together around a fire when Jesus suddenly begins to question Peter's love for Him—in front of everyone! I can imagine the pain in Peter's voice as he answered. I'm sure he was trying to prove his loyalty and love to the Lord, knowing his word shouldn't be trusted. Peter declared his love for Jesus three times, just as he denied Him three times. Jesus revealed the direct conflict in Peter's spoken word. Jesus knew about this unrest inside of Peter and was getting to the bottom of what was hurting him the most: his own fickle heart. Jesus asked Peter a question that probably hurt and embarrassed him. But behind this moment of confrontation, the truth came to light and Peter was set free from being defined by his temperamental, inconsistent words ever again. Jesus was telling Peter that *"Love is an action and not a word. It doesn't matter what you have done or said before; this is how you can love me from now on: Feed my sheep."*

From that place of love, from that place of security, and from that place of intimacy, Jesus calls us to be *His*

Love extended

to "feed His sheep."

Jesus sometimes asks us offensive questions to get to the root of those things that have captivated our heart other than Him. *Do you love me more than your success, security, career? Will you love me when you don't understand my ways? Will you love me when you don't see how my promise will come to pass?* The moment that Peter denied Jesus looked very grim. It appeared God's promises weren't going to pull through. But Jesus remained faithful anyway. As Jesus looked at Peter and said, "Do you love me?" He was in a way telling Peter: *"I'm here for you; now, the next time life looks grim, will you trust me?"* From that place of love, from that place of security, and from that place of intimacy, Jesus calls us to be *His love extended* to "feed His sheep."

The Last Mandate

The last mandate Jesus left us with before ascending to Heaven was to "Go into all the world and preach the Good News." That mandate has changed our lives and has the power to transform the planet. It's a beautiful conclusion to a beautiful love letter written to us and now to be lived out through us. My husband, Taylor, and I are currently serving as missionaries to unreached and under-reached people groups in the Amazon Jungle of Peru. We prepared to "go into all the world" by going to college and majoring in Biblical Studies and Global Missions. We also completed a one-year immersive mission's internship in Central America where we learned Spanish. God gave us a God-called vision to reach His Amazon Bride and to raise up an end-time army of missionaries. We love doing missions work for God's Kingdom. But it is important to understand that we are ALL called to extend the love of God. We can't all go to Peru or do global missions work, but we can ALL reach the one that lives next door. Let's live our lives answering this call to extend God's love, from a place of passionately and radically loving Jesus! I can hear Jesus even today, still saying, *"Until I come back for you, tell the world this love story I have shared with you! If you love me Beloved Bride, feed My sheep!"*

Ask Yourself:

Do you feel exempt from feeding God's sheep because of perceived "disqualifications?"

Is there a personal failure/shortcoming in your life that still needs redeeming like Peter needed from Jesus? Is it difficult to receive God's truth over a place in your past? If so, why?

When was the last time that you fed someone hungry with the love of Jesus? How did it make you feel?

What most often prevents you from evangelizing to those around you? How can you overcome that obstacle?

When is the last time you prayed a prayer of availability to go and do whatever God would call you to? Have you allowed any compromise to creep into your life?

Digging Deeper:

Read John 1:42. Peter was known for his emotional instability, yet when Jesus saw him for the first time, He changed his name from Simon to "Cephas" (translated: Peter—which means rock or stone).

Why do you think it was important for Jesus to change Simon Peter's name? What was the significance of it?

If Jesus were to give you a new name, what would it be and why?

According to John 21:15-17, Jesus asked Peter: "Do you love me more than these?" The "these" he is referring to is believed to be the 153 fish that Jesus had enabled them to catch earlier that day—signifying success and prosperity.

If Jesus was standing before you today, what would be the "these" He would be referring to in your life? Is there anything you are holding on to that you love more than Jesus?

Read John 18:1-27. Peter was convinced that Jesus was the Messiah they had all been waiting for. He had probably pictured Jesus being crowned and ruling and reigning over all of Israel as the King. He could most likely imagine Him wearing royal robes and living in the palace...but now he was on trial and people were crying "crucify him." When the story didn't play out in the same way he thought it should, he became so confused, hurt, and broken inside that his emotions got the best of him, and he denied Jesus three times when confronted about knowing him. At that time, Peter could not see the great love that Jesus was about to pour out. Love that was truly unrivaled. He could not see that God had a much greater plan—a plan that didn't just involve the believing Jews in Israel, but a plan that involved extending His love to all humankind.

In what way can you identify with Peter denying Jesus when he was not able to see/believe the resurrection that was in store?

In chapter 21, Jesus repeated the question "Do you love me?" three times. Most likely this puzzled Peter; it may have even hurt his feelings. But the Lord was actually showing great love and compassion for this disciple who had recently denied him. Jesus knew that even though Peter was emotionally enthusiastic, his commitment would not last if he was not confident in his love for Christ.

There are two Greek words used for love in this passage. The first was used the first two times Jesus asked the question, and the second kind of love was mentioned in the third question.

1. *Agape* speaks of an intelligent, thoughtful, and purposeful love involving the entire personality, but primarily a decision of the mind and will.
2. *Phileo* speaks of a warm, natural, and more spontaneous sense of feeling and affection. A more emotional love.

Through these two words, Jesus points out that Peter's love, and our love, must be more than a commitment of mind, but also of the heart. It must be a love motivated by both purpose and personal attachment.

What was the significance of Jesus asking Peter the confronting question "Do you love me?" three different times?

All of Christ's followers face the same question. The main issue is not "Are you willing to do anything for God?" or "Do you love others?" The primary question is this: "Do you really love ME (God)?" A deep love for God is the only effective motivation for serving Him and extending His love to the world.

Jesus knew the persecution that Peter would face when He was gone. Therefore, it is out of truly knowing Him, knowing we are loved by Him, and loving Him in relationship that we have the passion and power to fulfill our God-given purposes in life, no matter what we must endure along the way. (Fire Bible, NIV; p. 1971).

Do you feel that you are living in a place of overflow from your love relationship with God? If not, what is stopping you?

Read John 4:31-38. The disciples urged Jesus to eat, but Jesus begins to teach them a lesson. He said He had food that they knew nothing about. The disciples wondered if someone had brought Jesus some food that they were not aware of. Jesus explained that *His food* is to do the will of Him (God the Father) who had sent Him and to finish His work. He proceeded to talk to them about fields that are ripe for harvest.

What or who is the harvest? Who are the laborers? Why is the harvest great, but the laborers are few?

What is our role in reaping this eternal crop? Why is it referred to as an "eternal" crop?

Read Matthew 28:19-20. This Scripture passage is often called the "Great Commission." This was given as God's primary command, instruction, and missional task—along with the authority to carry it out. This command applies to all of His followers of every generation. In Jesus' final instructions, He states the goal and responsibility of His church (His local and worldwide community). They are to take His message and His love and extend it to the people of all nations and all cultures.

What did Jesus commission His disciples and all believers to do?

Therefore _____!
Make _____ of _____ nations!
Baptize them.
_____ them to obey everything I have commanded you.

"Therefore go...Make disciples of all nations... Baptize them...Teach them to obey everything I have commanded you!" (Matt. 28:19-20, NIV).

You may say, "But wait a minute. I am not a preacher or teacher or a missionary. I haven't been to Bible school and have hardly been out of my own city much less been on a mission's trip." That's OK. God knows that! And yet He poured His love out on you and He called YOU. With the same unrivaled love that we have been extended from our Bridegroom Jesus, we, His Bride, have the responsibility and awesome privilege to share it with the world around us.

In what ways has God specifically gifted/positioned you to share His love with those that are physically and spiritually hungry?

Are there specific people and places that God is calling you to go and extend His love? If so, what/who are they? If not, when is the last time you asked God and trusted Him to give you an answer?

Personal Application:

How can you intentionally position yourself to live a life that is overflowing with God's love?

List some practical ways that you can be God's love extended by "feeding His sheep."

What are some practical things that your Empowered sisterhood group (or your devotional group) can do to put activation to God's love?

Prayer Activation:

Lord,

I thank You for extending Your love to me. Fill me with Your love so much that I overflow in every capacity of my life. Teach me how to remain and abide in Your love every day so that I never run dry. Light up every hidden place in my heart and life with our Holy Spirit. Let me live according to the truth of the name You have given me and never answer to any other. And send me to Your hungry sheep, wherever they might be, and enable me to always have more than enough to give them.

Amen!

To my Chosen.

_____

(insert your name)

Demonstrate this same love I have for you by loving others (John 13:35 TPT) and make room in your heart to love every believer (Matthew 13:1 TPT). If you keep my commands, I promise you will remain in my love, just as I have kept my Father's commands and I have remained in His love (John 15:10 TPT).

Love Always,
Jesus

Love your neighbor
who doesn't look like you,
think like you, love like you,
speak like you, pray like you.

NO EXCEPTIONS!
Extend LOVE, Live LOVE.

My "Live Loved" Declarations

According to I Corinthians 13

I, _____, declare:

Love is patient and kind. (So am I).

Love cares more for others than for self. (So do I).

Love doesn't want what it doesn't have. (Neither do I).

Love doesn't strut. (Neither do I).

Love doesn't have a swelled head. (Neither do I).

Love doesn't force itself on others. (Neither do I).

Love isn't always "me first." (Neither am I).

Love doesn't fly off the handle. (Neither do I).

Love doesn't keep score of the sins of others. (Neither do I).

Love doesn't celebrate when others fail. (Neither do I).

Love takes pleasure in the flowering of truth. (So do I).

Love puts up with anything. (So do I).

Love trusts God always. (So do I).

Love always looks for the best. (So do I).

Love never looks back. (Neither do I).

Love keeps going to the end. (So do I).

GOD PASSIONATELY LOVES ME. (I know I am loved.)

He passionately loves the whosoever will of the world. (And so do I).

My Love Notes:

"Now is the time...

TO GO,
TO EMBRACE,
TO SPEAK WORDS THAT
NEED TO BE SPOKEN,
TO WEEP AND TO LAUGH…
TO PRAY TOGETHER AND
TO POUR OUT OUR HEARTS.
NOW IS THE TIME
TO **LOVE** BETTER THAN
WE HAVE EVER LOVED
BEFORE."

- BECKY BAUDOUIN

Love Songs:
SUGGESTED WORSHIP PLAYLIST

If you are looking for songs to go with each lesson, we have listed a few of our favorites just for you. These are beautiful songs that will create an atmosphere of worship for each session theme. You may want to download them for listening during your private time with the Lord, or you may want to use them in a worship or soaking service. Enjoy the presence of God as you join Him as ONE in His LOVE!

Session 1

Love: REDEFINES

SONG #1: HOW GREAT IS YOUR LOVE (PASSION)

SONG #2: EXTRAVAGANT (BETHEL MUSIC)

SONG #3: UNCONTAINABLE LOVE (ELEVATION WORSHIP)

SONG #4: REAL THING (VERTICAL WORSHIP)

SONG #5: OH WHAT LOVE (CITY HARMONIC)

Session 2

Love: CHOOSES

SONG #1: WHO YOU SAY I AM (HILLSONG)

SONG #2: HOLDING NOTHING BACK (JESUS CULTURE)

SONG #3: CONTROL - ACOUSTIC (TENTH AVENUE NORTH)

SONG #4: SONS AND DAUGHTERS (BRET STANFILL)

SONG #5: I CAN'T BELIEVE (ELEVATION WORSHIP)

Session 3

Love: RESTORES

SONG #1: O COME TO THE ALTAR (ELEVATION WORSHIP)

SONG #2: DANCING ON THE WAVES (WE THE KINGDOM)

SONG #3: CLEAN (NATALIE GRANT)

SONG #4: ALL THINGS NEW (HILLSONG WORSHIP)

SONG #5: WHAT MERCY DID FOR ME (CHARITY GAYLE FT. JOSHUA SHERMAN)

Session 4

Love: TRUSTS

SONG #1: HIS LOVE NEVER FAILS (JESUS CULTURE)

SONG #2: BE STILL (HILLSONG WORSHIP)

SONG #3: PRAISE BEFORE MY BREAKTHROUGH (BRYAN AND KATIE TORWALT)

SONG #4: IN CHRIST ALONE (PASSION)

SONG #5: YOU ALONE (NORTH POINT WORSHIP FT. LAUREN DAIGLE)

Session 5

Love: SERVES

SONG #1: CHILDREN OF LIGHT (REND COLLECTIVE)

SONG #2: FIRE FALL DOWN (HILLSONG UNITED)

SONG #3: SOUL ON FIRE (THIRD DAY FT. ALL SONS & DAUGHTERS)

SONG #4: WHOLE HEART (PASSION)

SONG #5: FREE AS A BIRD (REND COLLECTIVE)

Session 6

Love: WAITS

SONG #1: I WILL WAIT FOR YOU - PSALM 130 (SHANE & SHANE)

SONG #2: SEASONS (HILLSONG WORSHIP)

SONG #3: WAITING HERE FOR YOU (CHRISTY NOCKELS)

SONG #4: WHILE I WAIT (LINCOLN BREWSTER)

SONG #5: IT IS WELL (BETHEL MUSIC)

Session 7

Love: CONNECTS

SONG #1: WE ARE ONE (CITY HARMONIC)

SONG #2: ALL THE PEOPLE SAID AMEN (MATT MAHER)

SONG #3: WITH EVERY ACT OF LOVE (JASON GRAY)

SONG #4: MAKE US ONE - LIVE (JESUS CULTURE)

SONG #5: WE ARE ROYALS (NORTH POINT WORSHIP)

Session 8

Love: COVERS

SONG #1: JESUS I COME (ELEVATION WORSHIP)

SONG #2: PRAISE WILL BE MY SONG (BRYAN & KATIE TORWALT)

SONG #3: IT IS FINISHED - ACOUSTIC (PASSION)

SONG #4: GREATER THAN ALL MY REGRETS (TENTH AVENUE NORTH)

SONG #5: REDEEMED BY THE BLOOD OF THE LAMB (PEOPLE AND SONGS)

Session 9

Love: SHOWS-UP

SONG #1: CALL UPON THE LORD (ELEVATION)

SONG #2: MY CONFIDENCE (IRON BELL MUSIC)

SONG #3: I AM (INFLUENCE MUSIC)

SONG #4: GOODNESS OF GOD (BETHEL MUSIC)

SONG #5: ANOTHER IN THE FIRE (HILLSONG UNTIED)

Session 10

Love: LIFTS

SONG #1: GRATEFUL (ELEVATION WORSHIP)

SONG #2: HE WILL HOLD ME FAST (SHANE & SHANE)

SONG #3: LIFTER (HOUSEFIRES)

SONG #4: NEW SONG - PSALM 40 (THE DODDS)

SONG #5: CHRIST BE ALL AROUND ME (ALL SONS & DAUGHTERS)

Session 11

Love: GROWS

SONG #1: CHANGING ME (ANNA GOLDEN)

SONG #2: REVEAL YOURSELF (VINTAGE WORSHIP)

SONG #3: TOUCH OF HEAVEN (HILLSONG WORSHIP)

SONG #4: I WANT TO KNOW YOU (JESUS CULTURE)

SONG #5: FURTHER - LIVE (INFLUENCERS WORSHIP)

Session 12

Love: EXTENDS

SONG #1: FOR THIS PURPOSE - LIVE (SEU WORSHIP)

SONG #2: ON EARTH AS IN HEAVEN - LIVE (RED ROCKS WORSHIP)

SONG #3: THE CAUSE OF CHRIST (KARI JOBE)

SONG #4: YOU HAVE CALLED ME HIGHER (ALL SONS & DAUGHTERS)

SONG #5: LIVE LIKE THAT (SIDEWALK PROPHETS)

made WITH love

There is a special comfort in sharing a meal or a treat with a friend. Jesus often sat at the table and ate with those whom He loved and those whom He wanted to speak life and wisdom into. In the same manner it is nice to sit and eat with those we love and those whom we want to bless. We have shared a few of our favorite recipes that we love to share with our friends and family.

When you gather with your small group you might want to make the mushroom quiche; when you want to bless an ill friend with a hot meal you can cook them up the easy chicken casserole. When you sit one on one to mentor a sister, the blueberry tart would be perfect with a cup of coffee or hot tea. And when you want to bless several women in your sisterhood you might think about making the yummy spiced paeans or homemade chocolate chip cookies by putting them into individual gift bags as a wonderful gift ready to share.

EASY RITZ CRACKER CHICKEN CASSEROLE

Serves 5

INGREDIENTS

- 4 cups cooked chicken (fully cooked and shredded)
- 10.5 oz cream of chicken soup
- 1 cup sour cream
- 1/2 teaspoon onion powder
- 1/4 teaspoon garlic powder
- 1/4 teaspoon salt (or to taste)
- 1/8 teaspoon pepper (or to taste)
- 1 sleeve Ritz crackers (crushed)
- 6 tablespoons butter (melted)

INSTRUCTIONS

- Preheat your oven to 350 ºF.
- Prepare a casserole dish with non-stick cooking spray and set aside.
- Mix cooked and shredded chicken with cream of chicken soup, sour cream, and seasonings.
- Add to the bottom of your prepared casserole dish.
- Top your casserole with crushed crackers and melted butter.
- Bake for 20-30 minutes.

SPICED PECANS

INGREDIENTS

- 1 egg white, lightly beaten
- 1 tablespoon water
- 3 cups pecan halves
- ½ cup white sugar
- ½ teaspoon salt
- 1 teaspoon ground cinnamon
- ½ teaspoon ground cloves
- ½ teaspoon ground nutmeg

INSTRUCTIONS

- Preheat oven to 350 ºF.
- Line a baking sheet with aluminum foil
- In a small bowl beat the egg white with the water. Stir in the pecans, mixing until well moistened.
- In a small bowl, mix together sugar, salt, cinnamon, cloves, and nutmeg. Sprinkle over the moistened nuts.
- Spread the nuts on prepared pan.
- Bake in preheated oven for 30 minutes, stirring once or twice. Be careful not to overcook and burn the nuts.
- Let cool and serve in a large bowl, or divide out into smaller portions and put into small bags to give to friends as a special gift.

What meal or dessert feels like love?

_____

_____

_____

_____

BLUEBERRY MASCARPONE TART

Serves 10

INGREDIENTS

- 1½ cups all-purpose flour
- ½ cup powdered sugar
- 1 tsp. lemon zest
- 1 tsp. orange zest
- ½ tsp. Salt
- 1½ sticks (¾ cup) butter, cut into 1-inch pieces
- ½ cup heavy cream
- 6 tbsp. powdered sugar
- ½ cup mascarpone cheese
- 1 tsp. lemon zest
- 1 tsp. lemon juice
- 3 cups fresh blueberries

INSTRUCTIONS

- For crust, in a food processor combine flour, ½ cup powdered sugar, 1 tsp. lemon zest, orange zest, and salt. Pulse to combine. Add butter. Process just until mixture comes together and forms a ball.
- Press dough into an 8x11-nch rectangular tart pan with removable bottom; press dough all the way up edges of tart pan. Chill 20 minutes.
- Preheat oven to 350ºF. bake tart shell 18-20 minutes or until golden brown. Cool on a wire rack.
- For filling, in a bowl beat cream and the 6 tbsp. powered sugar with a mixer on medium until soft peaks form (tips curl).
- Add mascarpone cheese, 1 tsp. lemon zest, and lemon juice. Beat until combined.
- Pour filling into cooled tart shell. Top with blueberries. Chill up to 24 hours.
- Remove tart from pan and cut into piece.

PORTOBELLO MUSHROOM QUICHE

Serves 8

INGREDIENTS

- 1 Partially Baked Pastry Crust
- 2 tbsp. butter
- 2 cups sliced baby portobello or cremini mushrooms
- ½ cup thinly sliced green onions
- 1 clove garlic, minced
- 1 cup baby spinach
- 6 eggs
- 1½ cups heavy cream
- ½ tsp. salt
- ½ tsp black pepper
- ¼ tsp. grated fresh nutmeg
- 1 cup shredded Swiss cheese (4 oz.)

INSTRUCTIONS

- Prepare the Partially Baked Pastry Crust, *below*.
- Reduce oven temperature to 325ºF.
- In a large skillet melt butter over medium-high. Add the mushrooms, green onions, and garlic. Cook and stir about 6 minutes or until mushrooms are tender.
- Stir in spinach until slightly wilted.
- Whisk to lightly beat the eggs in a large bowl. Whisk in cream, salt, pepper, and nutmeg. Stir in Swiss cheese and mushroom mixture. Pour into crust.
- Bake about 50 minutes or until quiche is puffed and golden. Let cool 10 minutes on a wire rack before serving. Cut quiche into wedges.

PARTIALLY BAKED PASTRY CRUST

- Preheat oven to 450 ºF.
- Line a 9-inch pie plate with homemade pastry for a single-crust pie or one rolled refrigerated unbaked piecrust.
- Line pastry with foil. Bake for 8 minutes. Remove foil. Bake 4 to 5 minutes more or until crust is set and dry.

CHOCOLATE CHIP COOKIES

By: Mary Price

Yields 3 dozen

INGREDIENTS

- ¾ Cup of Crisco/shortening
- 1 ¼ Cups of dark brown sugar (packed)
- 2 Tablespoons of milk
- 1 Tablespoon of vanilla
- 1 Egg
- 2 Cups of flour
- 1 teaspoon of salt
- ¾ teaspoon of baking soda
- 6 oz of milk chocolate chips
- 1 Cup of chopped pecans

INSTRUCTIONS

- Preheat oven to 375 ºF.
- Beat shortening, brown sugar, milk and vanilla in large bowl with mixer until well blended. Beat in egg.
- Combine flour, salt and baking soda. Mix into shortening mixture until blended.
- Stir in chocolate chips and nuts.
- Measure tablespoonfuls of dough and drop 3 inches apart onto a baking sheet.
- Bake 8-10 minutes.

SHARE OTHER YUMMY RECIPES THAT YOU LOVE WITH THE GIRLS IN YOUR EMPOWERED SISTERHOOD!

EMPOWERED GIVING:
Alabaster Box

Join Empowered Women's Ministries in caring for the poor, the orphaned, and the forgotten.

Empowered Women's Ministries is a nonprofit Christ-centered movement that cares for the vulnerable and forgotten in the United States and around the world, and seeks to encourage and equip women to live an empowered life through Christ. Supporting Projects:

GIRL *Talk*

RESCUE HER

IMPACT APPALACHIA

AHIKAM
Guatemala Orphanage

And much more:
- Pastors Kids of Deceased Parents
- Missionaries Worldwide
- Resource and Leadership Development

Just as Mary took her alabaster box filled with costly oil and anointed the feet of Jesus, we too can give our best to show our love for Christ.

SHE LEADS:

Leadership Development

FEEL CALLED TO LEAD? Empowered Women's Ministries and the PENTECOSTAL CHURCH OF GOD are glad to introduce quality training for ministry through IMC MINISTRY MULTIPLICATION.

FORERUNNER EXPERIENCE

//12 Weeks Designed to Simplify and Speed Up Your Journey into Ministry//

Targeted to those 17-30 years of age
For more information: *forerunner.pcg.org*

MINISTRY INTENSIVES

//Yearlong Training to Advance New Ministry, Broaden Existing Ministry, and Equip You to Walk Worthy of Your Calling//

Attend the on-campus experience in Bedford, Texas, for a week of quality teaching intensives.
Includes an available track on "Women In Ministry"
For more information: *pcg.org/intensives*

MESSENGER COLLEGE

//Committed to Developing World-Changing Pentecostal Leaders for the 21st Century//

Messenger College offers a fully accredited bachelor's or associate degree. For your convenience, you can choose to attend live classes at our Bedford, Texas campus or take online classes.
For more information: *messengercollege.edu*

EMPOWERED RESOURCES:
Companion Devo's & more...

UNLIMITED:
POWER OF ONE
(Connecting with God and Others)

Book 1 of 3 in the devotional study series.
Released 2019

$12.99

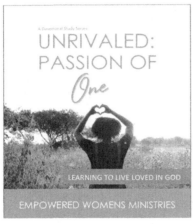

UNRIVALED:
PASSION OF ONE
(Learning to Live Loved in God)

Book 2 of 3 in the devotional study series.
Released 2020

$12.99

Soon to be released in Spanish.

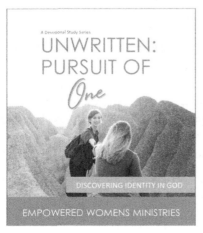

UNWRITTEN:
PURSUIT OF ONE
(Discovering Identity in God)

Book 3 of 3 in the devotional study series.
To be released January 2021

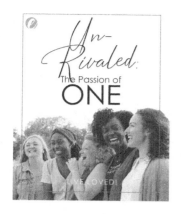

UNRIVALED: The Passion of ONE- LIVE *loved!*

Graphics available through Empowered Women's Ministries.

SEE: *www.pcg.org/women* for free downloadable theme graphics which, can be used to make posters, cards, name tags, and more. Great to promote your study group, a yearly theme, or a women's conference.

ONE IN THE BELOVED

This 21- Day Devotional is a beautiful study guide on the disciplines of prayer, fasting, and solitude. A perfect companion study to go alongside *UNRIVALED: Passion of ONE*, or any of the Devotional Books in the ONE series.

By Jenni Gilbert

Available for FREE digital download at *pcg.org/21days*

"EMPOWERED" T-SHIRT

SHORT SLEEVE- Women's Fit
V-neck T-Shirt by Bella (black).
Sizes S–XL $20.00

"LIVE *loved*" Empowered Women's Logo

LONG SLEEVE- Extra soft T-Shirt by Bella (picture shows front and back: comes in steel blue and heathered mauve).
Sizes S–XXL $24

TO ORDER, Please Contact:
empoweredwmin@pcg.org or 817-554-5900 ext. 370

EMPOWERED WOMEN'S MINISTRIES

connection

I-Connect provides the opportunity for PCG women to join hearts and hands with **Empowered Women's Ministries.** We value your voice in our community of faith and your desire to help us as we advance the Kingdom of God **together as one.**

TO REGISTER:
Provide a $5.00 membership fee to:
EMPOWERED WOMEN'S MINISTRIES
2701 Brown Trail, Bedford, TX 76021
or CONTACT: *empoweredwmin@pcg.org*

AN EMPOWERED CONNECT MEMBERSHIP PROVIDES:

- A full one-year membership.
- A one-year monthly subscription to our "Empower Her" e-newsletter filled with empowering articles, Scripture focus, outreach projects, and much more.
- Prayer from your local, district and national leaders.
- Discounts on PCG national and district designated resources, retreats, and conferences.
- Support help for furthering ministry to women in the local church and around the world.
- A connected voice and sisterhood with thousands of other Pentecostal Church of God women around the country.

EMPOWERED WOMEN'S MINISTRIES is an active ministry of dedicated women of the Pentecostal Church of God. Thousands of women are inspired and motivated by the ministry through prayer, support, and outreach endeavors.

The women's ministry operates under the organizational structure of the Pentecostal Church of God on local church, state/district, national, and international levels.

Empowered Women's Ministries exist to represent Jesus Christ throughout the earth. By the power of the Holy Spirit, our mission is to evangelize, disciple, encourage, and equip women to live the Empowered life in Christ.

TO FIND OUT MORE ABOUT
EMPOWERED WOMEN'S MINISTRIES
AND THE PENTECOSTAL CHURCH OF GOD
CHECK OUT

pcg.org/women

FOLLOW @empoweredwomensministries on

empowered
WOMEN'S MINISTRIES
PENTECOSTAL CHURCH OF GOD

FOR ORDER INFORMATION, PLEASE VISIT
pcg.org/women
or contact us at
empoweredwmin@pcg.org
817-554-5900 ext. 370

Made in the USA
Middletown, DE
12 January 2020